It's Not
About
Love

(at least not the way you think)

Congratulations — you've
found a free copy
signed by the author.
Read and enjoy!

James

Published in Canada, for Global Distribution
by YGTMedia Co.
www.ygtmedia.co/publishing
To order additional copies of this book:
publishing@ygtmedia.co

Edited by Rachel Small and Christine Stock
Book design by Doris Chung
Cover design by Michelle Fairbanks
ePub by Ellie Sipilä

Printed in North America

It's Not About Love

(at least not the way you think)

JAMIE MURRAY

CFO & AUTHOR OF
HOW MANY KIDS DO YOU HAVE?

Table of Contents

Benediction

May grace always remind us

If not for the experiences, we wouldn't have had the struggles.
If not for the struggles, we wouldn't have had the growth.
If not for the growth, we wouldn't have our perspectives.
If not for our perspectives, we wouldn't be able to forgive.
If not for forgiveness, we couldn't love ourselves.
If we couldn't love ourselves, we could never love anyone else.

Author's Note

I've come to accept that we can never know exactly why another person does what they do. We can analyze, hypothesize, rationalize—and be left with only more questions. What I've come to appreciate is that each of us is only ever living our own life.

The truth we all hide from is that we're ultimately doing life on our own. People may walk on paths beside ours, but we're on our own path. Generally, we call the people walking alongside us our family. Our family structure can change any number of times in a lifetime. Some of our family members support us, others do not. Still, we are only ever living our own life.

Our families help to mold our experiences, our values, and our priorities, so it's easy for members of a family to forget they came together as individuals. The melding of lives is why it's so hard to let go of our children when they're ready to fly.

And why a broken partnership can bring us to our knees.

Introduction

I wrote a book about the hardships of blended families based on my experiences over the course of ten years of marriage. I ended said book on a high note, reflecting on how much progress our blended family had made. Six days after that book was released, I found out my husband was cheating on me.

I released the book on a Tuesday. I celebrated and had plans and goals and hope for my future. By Monday, my marriage had crumbled and I was left holding a book about a family I no longer had.

The road has been difficult since that day. I'm not here to tell anyone what to do, or that there's some easy path to recovery, or that forgiveness is necessary. My intention is much like the one behind my first book: I'm simply here to say out loud what so many of us are managing in silence. Maybe this book can help you cope a little better on your journey. But your journey is most definitely your own.

This book is about a lot of things. It's about what happens in the aftermath of events that bring us to our knees. It's about how we can manage when the ground shifts beneath us, and how we can maneuver through our human journey when we feel broken.

It's about how turning toward spirituality can help ground us in the most unsolid of times. It's about learning to love ourselves. It's about walking through difficult moments and deciding who we want to be when it's all said and done.

It's also about infidelity. If it weren't, I wouldn't be speaking my truth very well. Do the lessons extend to more than one kind of hurt or betrayal? Good lord I hope so, or else I've just put a lot of energy into a shortsighted message. This book is about cheating, but that's not all it has to offer. My hope is that this book is about how we manage in times of personal crisis, how we continue to love people even when they've hurt us, and how we learn to set and enforce necessary boundaries.

This book isn't about the lurid details of infidelity, or even whether a marriage can be salvaged afterwards. This book is about the broke-open moments in life—about the earth-shattering blows we thought would break us but instead just broke us open. I'm not going to give you all the answers you need in your own life or lay down a list of expectations or tell you it's all going to be okay. I'm going to walk you through my journey, my epiphanies, my growth, in hopes that my story heals you too in some small way.

Life is messy. We humans find ways to make it messier. Daily. I could gloss over the cringy parts, I could avoid the truths that were once too hard to acknowledge, I could skip over the weight of the hurt. I could, but it wouldn't help me or anyone else.

Instead, I'm going to tell my story with pride and self-love because, in the end, it's just another story about humanity. I'm not special, you're not special, no one person matters any more than another, regardless of what some may preach. This is my story but also my mother's story, my father's story, my neighbor's story, my coworker's story, my best friend's story, my mentor's story, my children's story, and so on. It's a story about how we find a way to learn what it means to love ourselves.

Do I want you, in turn, to speak your story? That, my dear, has nothing to do with me. This is your journey, your life here on earth, your choices. No one else gets to decide what's right for you—not me, not a partner, not a child, not a parent. No one else gets to tell you how to feel and react in your story. The point here is to read, feel, learn, grow, change. This book is meant to encourage you to be guided by your own instincts and life knowledge, to empower you to heal your past and present hurts. Take your time, move when you're ready, heal, sleep, read, take a time-out. You don't have to keep up with anyone else. Not even the people under your own roof. The more centered you are, the more clarity you gain, the more peace you find within, the more you can trust yourself, the more you can love yourself. That's what it's all about.

I'm a researcher at heart. When crises happen, I go into researcher mode. I read, podcast, Audible, MasterClass, and Google the shit out of a topic until I feel as if I know it inside and out. My kids groan every time they get in the car with me, fully aware of the self-help BS awaiting them on their ride to school (I think they secretly listen sometimes, but please don't tell them I know that). I've always been this way. If I can prove I'm not the only one going through hard moments (and they are only moments, after all), I can feel a little more okay while managing life. When I know others have made it through, I feel more confident I can too.

One of my favorite guides is author and strategic life coach Leisse Wilcox, who coined the term "Emotional Alchemy" in her first book, *To Call Myself Beloved*. Wilcox explains that to perform Emotional Alchemy is to "take something dark, ugly and unwanted, and turn it into something beautiful, golden and uniquely your own."[1] This story starts with cheating, but it's really a story about learning to love yourself.

Before you go rushing to your kitchen to get another glass of vino to drown out this woo-woo hippy psychobabble, just wait. "True self-love," says Wilcox, "is the ability to look in the mirror, meet the person you are going to spend the rest of your life with, and feel total appreciation for that person looking back at you." When the bottom fell out of my life, I certainly didn't feel total appreciation for myself. Still, I held tight to the idea of Emotional Alchemy and the belief that I could manage this life crisis without allowing it to define me. "Choose love over fear," Wilcox writes.

Of course, that's easier said than done. Please don't confuse choosing love over fear with being a doormat or staying in a situation that holds you back from who you're meant to be. Choose love over fear when it comes to the relationship with yourself. I came to understand that the infidelity in my marriage wasn't about me, about how much my spouse loved me, or about how much of our life was based on lies. Don't get me wrong, these are significant questions, but they weren't questions that could be answered. They weren't the questions that were going to get me through to the other side as a whole and loving person.

I eventually accepted that the reason my spouse could lie to me, could compartmentalize a life outside of the one we were living together, could uphold the farce he was living, was that he couldn't love himself. From there, I had to decide how I was going to avoid the same fate. How was I going to love myself? How was I going to keep the betrayal from turning me into a person I didn't want to be? How was I going to manage the tsunami of emotions I was going through daily?

I wrote this book mostly to answer those questions for myself.

Just when I'd hit my stride in healing, flashbacks would ravage my mind, tearing off the barely formed scabs around my hurt. One or fifteen triggers would come along to sideswipe me again. The early days and months after uncovering infidelity can feel tortuous. So, in an effort to stay grounded, I increased the number of counseling sessions

I was attending, I put down the wine and whiskey, and I vowed to write my way through it.

When I wrote my first book, I wanted to change the conversation about blended families and how we maneuver heartache and loyalty and marriage and parenting. I wrote this second book in hopes of changing the conversation around marital infidelity and how we maneuver heartache and loyalty and marriage and parenting.

I also wrote this book with my children in mind. When I'm not here, and they're navigating adulthood on their own, what will they remember? How will they tell the story of our family? What questions will they be seeking answers to from their past, so that they can create a future that works for them? I know I can't guarantee them a life without heartache—if anything, I can guarantee they'll experience heartache. But my words will be with them, so they will never feel alone.

What you hold here is my contribution to the conversation about how we learn to love ourselves. It's what I've learned, what I'm still struggling to learn, and what we can all do to practice Emotional Alchemy.

SECTION ONE

The Break

When one is pretending, the entire body revolts.

–Anaïs Nin

Why in the Hell

Why in the hell would anyone be willing to put such a personal story out into the world? To air their dirty laundry? To put their trauma on display?

You must have been asking yourself these questions. Or maybe you weren't. Maybe I was. My answer is that the process of writing this book was extremely healing for me. And if I'm healing, my family is better off.

Also, I believe we shouldn't go through the really hard shit alone.

Writing helps me think and feel. To me, writing is like having a conversation with my oldest and dearest friends. In fact, I'm pretty sure I became an author because my best friend became a mother later in life, after my children were nearly grown. As I was taking my brain back, hers was just starting to be ravaged by her own precious little souls. In the midst of our being in two very different stages of life, writing became my way of talking to her whenever I needed. Sometimes while writing this book, I'd text her and explain that I was about to send her fifty text messages. "I don't need you to read them or reply," I'd say, because I knew she was literally chasing two toddlers around all day long. "I just need to feel as if I'm talking to you, so I can make sense of what I'm thinking and feeling."

When I write, I feel as if I'm part of those war-time-era romances where a character is sending twenty-four-page handwritten letters confessing their deepest secrets to a human they hardly know—a near stranger who won't see what they've written until well after they've written it.

The point is, I'm not writing to nobody. I'm not out here talking to myself. Writing exposes us to critique, judgment, shame, and even hate. Not everyone in my extended family loves that I've written books about my family. Still, I write because of those people, not despite them. Because not everyone will be my people, and that's okay. Not everyone will process my words as I intended them, and that's okay. Not everyone will see my insight as the harrowing, life-altering, visionary masterpiece that it is, and that's okay. Honestly, the critics around me don't have anything on the critic inside me. The naysayers, the onlookers, the judges—they can't ever hurt me like I've hurt myself.

I set out to write a book about infidelity, but I accidentally wrote a book about learning how to love myself. I know I'm not the only one dealing with this specific trauma, so I stand in front of you with a peace offering. A message. A call to action. Let's learn to love ourselves so that we might better love the ones around us. You might take something away from this book, and you might not. This might have to do with how I've put the words together, or it might have to do with where you are in your journey. Still, I'll reach out. I'll try. I'll live openly, honestly, and without fear, in hopes you feel you can do the same.

I hear the voice again. *Why in the hell would you put this story out into the world?* I peruse my bookshelves and see James Baldwin's novel *Giovanni's Room*. I see Maya Angelou's *I Know Why the Caged Bird Sings*, Amy Tan's *Saving Fish from Drowning*, Gloria Anzaldúa's *Borderlands/La Frontera*, Elizabeth Gilbert's *Eat Pray Love,* and Chelsea Hander's *Life Will Be the Death of Me*. I see Jenny Lawson's *Broken (In the Best Possible Way)*, in which she candidly normalizes mental health and lack thereof. I'm reminded that I'm not alone. I'm so grateful for every brave artist who put their own story on display for me and my growth and my healing. It must have been scary to do so.

These creators must have questioned why in the hell they were putting their words into the world. Why they were risking the backlash of exposure. When I remember the masterful creatives who came before me, the vulnerability they offered up freely to the world, I feel brave enough to try. To try to heal from it, to help put words to my shadow. To try to minimize the shame and self-doubt that exist in us all.

Telling our secrets leaves us no choice but to be exposed to the judgment and criticism of others. But what's more important is whether we're judging and criticizing ourselves.

Going through childhood with a mentally unstable parent, I grew up feeling as if the world were watching me. People were always staring, sizing us up, wondering what the hell to make of me, my father, my home. My father was forever talking to himself in stores in hopes someone would engage with him so he could carry on a loud, lengthy conversation. He demanded attention when he didn't get it. Suffice to say, passersby were always looking at us—judging him, pitying me. I often found myself inching away from him, humiliated by my reflection on other people's faces. I grew up feeling on display and embarrassed. I was the "trailer trash" on the school bus route, the often-disheveled, unkempt little girl who wore discount-store clothes and had uncombed hair. I was the seventeen-year-old waddling around my high school nine months pregnant. It's always felt as if the world were judging me.

Since the release of my first book, I've been asked, "How were you able to be so open? Were you scared to share so many potentially embarrassing parts of yourself with the world?" My answer is that I simply assume I'm not the only person in the world feeling these things. Going through hard stuff. Often unsure of how to maneuver through it all.

I'm proud of who I am today, of the human I've become, of the work

I've put into becoming me. I can put myself out there, all vulnerable and raw, because somewhere along the way in my forty-two years of this life, I stopped giving a shit about what the critics think. Hell, I'm sure I've thought most of it myself, so I don't even blame them.

I have friends who don't always appreciate my frankness, family members who critique me for being so open, acquaintances who say things behind my back, loved ones who think I should keep my mouth shut. But I'm not the only person to face infidelity in their marriage. I'm not the only person who has suffered from the trauma of betrayal. So rather than seek connections in my limited backyard with people who don't want to be open and honest and raw about the journey of life we're all on, I'm writing this book and letting it guide me to like-minded people all over the world.

In the fetal stages of writing this book, a good friend told me that the chapters would be my wounds but the book would be my healing. I couldn't have understood then just how right she'd be. Writing about something feels like laying a problem at the altar of God. I know it hasn't disappeared, I know it will still follow me, but I feel lighter and more capable of dealing with it. Writing through a storm changes the reality from which I view it. I may not have created it, I certainly have no control over it, and it's most definitely going to sweep me up in its wrath. Still, once the sun comes back out, once the chaos has settled, once the pain subsides, I will rebuild.

The world is bigger than what I see and live every day. I know there are many brave souls willing to speak about hardships so that others might heal and reclaim their lives. In all honesty, what do we have to lose? We can only come out stronger, better, and more experienced. My bubble is limited, but the world is not.

I live with my head held high because while I'm not perfect and people may not always "get" me, I'm only ever being me. That's something my dad taught me well. Fuck the world and live in your own, proudly and boldly.

It's Not About Love

Women are gaslit every single day. We buy a lot of the bullshit—about our world, our lives, and ourselves. Politicians break promises daily, the beauty industry tells us to hate our aging bodies, our bosses manipulate our efforts for their self-serving agendas, and our spouses sometimes create their own versions of reality and call us crazy when questioned. Hell, even motherhood can make the best of us question what we feel to be true.

When the world works to tear down the divine inside us, we can slowly melt into the background. Every so often the curtain is drawn back and we see the wizard behind it, pulling our strings. Superpowers reactivated, instincts momentarily restored, we go into flight AND fight mode, bringing our truths back to light. We pack, we move, we cry, we feel, we focus, we leave, we run, we fight back. We create change. But we can only run at such a pace for so long before we collapse. Bodies exhausted and souls bruised, we lie down to hibernate once more. We eat again, we linger again, we accept again. We allow our goals, our desires, and our energy to be derailed again. We stop loving ourselves.

This is why *it's not about love.*

Maybe it was the decades spent reading self-help books or the years spent in therapy, but I understood quickly that the infidelity in my marriage wasn't about me. My spouse's choices weren't a reflection of how much he did or didn't love me. His choices reflected how much he didn't love himself. And my denial throughout his affair reflected how much I didn't love myself.

It's easy to get lost in the thought spirals that tell us such betrayal means they never really loved us, they weren't getting what they needed, we can only hate each other now, our entire life was a lie, they must be a narcissist, people never change, we'll never be able to trust again, etc. But like most things in life, cheating isn't as complex as we make it. We'd like cheating to be more complicated so that it justifies the tailspin into which it sends our lives, but cheating is simple. All the lies and sneaking around, the compartmentalizing and the disloyalty—it stems from an inability to love yourself. The behaviors that allow for cheating, lying, or betrayal of any kind are a result of being unable to accept yourself for who you are. Someone who causes a loved one intentional harm doesn't believe they are worthy of love. They don't believe they deserve it. That's it.

I hear you disagreeing. "Oh, they love themselves all right. They love only themselves." That's not unconditional self-love. At the heart of it, when a loved one betrays us, the lies they tell everyone are simply masks for the lies they're telling themselves.

Love is frequently used as a crutch. The myth of idyllic love is often the reason we accept someone's ill treatment of us, whether it's an abusive parent, a cheating spouse, or an unhealthy sibling. How many times have we heard or said, "But I love them"; "They love me"; "They're family, I can't just walk away"; "Love will keep us together"; "Love is enough"; "Love is all we need." Actually, it isn't. Love isn't all you need. Humans need a variety of emotions to grow and flourish. Love is only one of the things we need. It certainly isn't enough to continue accepting subpar behaviors from people in our lives.

We all hear voices telling us that we aren't good enough, that we'll never amount to anything. "Who are you to believe you deserve more?" We simply handle it in different ways. Some eat too much, some don't eat enough, some run, some smoke, some drink, some lie, some cheat, some hate. It's just that when someone eats and smokes their fears and insecurities away, it typically has a less immediate impact on those around them. When someone drinks, lies, and cheats their fears and insecurities away, the collateral damage drastically increases.

It's not about love because setting boundaries rooted in what's best for us has absolutely nothing to do with how much we love someone, or how much they love us. The infidelity in my marriage had nothing to do with whether my husband loved me. It had nothing to do with me—I wasn't the one cheating.

We can all agree that long-term partnerships have ups and downs. They have cold seasons in which partners pull away from each other, and periods when one partner carries the other. I'm not suggesting that when it comes to problems in a marriage, there aren't two sides to the story. I'm saying that cheating is *always* about the person doing the cheating and not the one being cheated on. If I've already pissed you off, try to hear me out.

Infidelity involves lies, deception, and an overall lack of respect. When someone purposely hides part of themselves, lies to themselves to justify their actions, or actively deceives the most important humans in their life, it has everything to do with that person and nothing to do with the person it happens to.

It's not about love because betrayal isn't a reflection of how much someone does or doesn't love us. Infidelity isn't a reflection of whether your partner loves you. I'll say it one more time for the back row: Someone cheating on you isn't a reflection of whether they love you.

Just because someone *never* cheated on you doesn't mean they love you. It follows suit that just because someone cheats on you doesn't mean they don't love you. The point here is that how we handle infidelity shouldn't be rooted in whether we feel a partner really loves us. Full disclosure: it doesn't matter. When managing life after infidelity, hurt, or betrayal, whether someone loved you is the least relevant question to be asking yourself. A more productive question is, Do they love themselves?

It's not about love because if someone hasn't learned to love themselves, they won't be able to show love to anyone else. In the throes of betrayal, it's easy to get lost in semantics: "If you did this, you must not love me" or "If you loved me, you wouldn't have done this." If we're to maintain emotional stability after being betrayed, we must move beyond the question of whether someone loves us. Without even knowing you, the answer is most likely yes. Yes, your partner did love you. Perhaps does love you. It's just that it doesn't matter. A lack of love isn't why your partner cheated on you. Okay, well, that's not entirely true. A lack of love *is* actually why your partner cheated on you. It just wasn't because of a lack of love for *you*. Your partner cheated on you because of a lack of love for *themselves*.

It's not about love because people who love us can also make hurtful choices. Just because someone loves us doesn't mean they won't hurt us. Just because they hurt us doesn't mean they don't love us.

It's not about love when you set and enforce boundaries so you can fulfill your own soul's journey. You must make choices about what's best for you.

It's not about love when you decide who you want to be after a defining life event.

It's not about love for them—it's about how much you love yourself.

Recognizing the distinction between a person *not loving us* and a person *not loving themselves* is critical in the healing process. Whether you've been left, are leaving, or are sticking around, healing after a betrayal will need to take place. After we've been hurt, regardless of the next life chapter, we owe it to ourselves to proactively take steps toward healing so that we don't get stuck emotionally in the traumatic event—possibly one of the most traumatic events of our lives.

Once I fully felt into the idea that my partner's cheating wasn't my fault and had nothing to do with how much he loved me, I found more mental peace. When I set down my feelings of shame and stupidity, I found a way to love myself a little more. Was the marriage perfect? Far from it. Did the marriage need to grow? Absolutely. But if one partner can find a way to grow inside a marriage without lying and deceiving, why can't the other?

Here's where some of you stop liking me: people who cheat are broken on the inside. Maybe we all are in some ways, but a person who can't or won't control themselves when it comes to the actions required to cheat on a partner is a specific kind of broken. Since we now know their actions aren't about whether they love us but about whether they love themselves, we can set that hurt free a little more easily.

Those who lie and deceive the ones they love might love their ego, but they don't love themselves in an unconditional and self-accepting way. Barring people with emotional disorders, someone cannot feel good about who they are while they're deceiving and manipulating their loved ones. Their cheating is a manifestation of wounds left untreated. It's repetitive, I know, but it really does all come down to their inability to love themselves.

The freedom that comes from understanding that someone can

love us and still hurt us allows us to make better choices for ourselves and our families. If we believe everything was a lie, it's a lot harder to move forward. If we understand that someone's love for us isn't the defining factor in their choices, we can steady the emotional eruptions that follow betrayal. We can better manage our responses. We can be gaslit less frequently. When we take love out of the equation, we can manage our daily life in a more balanced way. We can hold love while also maintaining the boundaries necessary to heal ourselves.

There is freedom in accepting that you didn't cause the cheating in your relationship. There is comfort in knowing you likely weren't being duped the whole time by someone who never loved you, or that every real moment wasn't being faked, or that it wasn't all smoke and mirrors. Closer to the truth is that the happy moments were still happy. The love was still love. You don't have to doubt the good parts. They were real.

It's hard to believe. I know. Just remember: It's not about how much someone loves us but how much they love themselves. The good moments were real. They did exist, and you don't need to feel shame because the person you were sharing them with was broken on the inside.

Foreshadowing Our Lives

If it's true that we create the circumstances our souls desire for their journeys here on earth, then I most certainly should have seen this coming. I should have seen the foreshadowing in my own life. After all, it was in print—right in front of my face. I wrote in my first book that I didn't believe in love at first sight until I met my husband. I've since learned that instantly falling in love with someone and believing you're soulmates is a major sign of awful things to come. Turns out that an immediate addiction to someone isn't an indicator of a super-healthy future together. Who knew!

I referred to my husband as, and I quote my stupid ass, my "not-yet-reformed-bad-boy." Ouch. It's not always fun being right. I later read the book *F*ck Feelings*, written by father and daughter duo Michael Bennett and Sarah Bennett. In it, they explain that "a trained bear is still a bear, and a loved person with impairments is still impaired." They go on to say that "as temping as it might be, don't think of love as an instrument of improvement or redemption. Don't measure love's strength by its ability to turn a bad boy into the dream man."[2] While I'd like to believe that if I'd only read their book earlier, I could have learned to set better boundaries and see my own worth, I feel confident I wouldn't have done either of those things.

I also wrote about how my marriage would never end: "Until death do we part, mother fucker." If you've never experienced the sting of having your words coming back to haunt you, let me say it's a humbling experience, to say the least. I fought for this specific line. My first book had an ample number of cuss words, but my publisher and editors, while supportive of the artist's creative mind, still had a business to run. And so, I came to appreciate that maybe I didn't need quite so many f-bombs in a book about family (although that pretty much sums up my family of origin). When this specific f-bomb was in question, though, I fought for it, offering to remove others, because "until death do we part" just seemed sad on its own. Weak somehow. "Until death do we part, mother fucker" implied that we weren't getting out of this commitment unscathed. Being right never hurt so much.

We can usually see the writing on the wall—we just choose to ignore it. Why do we do this to ourselves? Excuse the sports analogy (once a basketball mom, always a basketball mom), but why do we call our shot and then act as if we didn't see the ball fall in the basket? Why are we so willing to overlook and excuse the very traits that will be our demise a decade or two from now? Why do we feel so blindsided? Why do we ignore the foreshadowing and then act as though we didn't see it coming when everything caves in on us?

We did see it coming. We knew he drank a little too much. We knew sometimes he said things a little too harsh for our comfort level. We knew we weren't to blame for his behaviors. Still, we loved him so much that we were willing to excuse and ignore behaviors that were beneath us. Behaviors that will impact how we feel about ourselves and the path our life will take. We really ought to pay more attention to the foreshadowing.

As the fog of blame began to lift, I came to the jarring realization that my husband had been battling demons I knew nothing about. I'd written about the patterns and cycles our blended family had faced over the years—I just hadn't yet recognized the marital cycles we were also facing. I'd written about how hard it was for him to reconcile years of abuse at the hands of a stepfather, and how becoming a stepfather resurrected all his childhood insecurities. I didn't account for the ways in which shame and self-hatred would manifest themselves in his ability to love himself. He loved us always. He just wasn't ever taught how to love himself.

Foreshadowing forces recognition. When betrayal strikes, we may be angry because some part of us either saw it coming or wasn't that surprised by it. When our souls are unsettled, disconnected, out of touch, we generally know what we aren't yet ready to say out loud. We don't want to know it, and we certainly don't allow ourselves to believe it, so we shut down the parts of our soul trying to speak our truths. We silence ourselves when we aren't brave enough to face the answers, and then we shame ourselves for not being open enough to see what was right under our noses. It's a self-sabotage cycle.

It's so easy to stop listening to your gut, stop trusting yourself, stop believing in your recollection of events. So how do we get back in touch with ourselves? I do it through writing. When I write, I find out things I didn't know I knew. Writing allows my hands to carry the load, so that my mind can take a break. If I just let my hands move through the words, I can almost always write myself out of a mood, a moment, a feeling. Each of us needs to find that thing for ourselves. Each of us needs to identify the space in which we're reacquainted with our intuition.

For my husband, it's golf. He can enter the flow state through a golf swing and reconnect to his body and soul on a golf course. My oldest son feels it when he shoots a basketball, my youngest son when he has a baseball glove on, and my daughters when they're racing horses. Find out what it is for you. What allows you to believe in yourself again and trust your gut? Sitting on a dock fishing? Taking a walk in a busy city? Watching a sunset from a rocking chair on a front porch? Calling friends and relatives every Sunday morning?

Figure out what puts you back in touch with your body and soul and then make time for that thing. Otherwise you may miss the fore-shadowing in your life.

Third-Date Conversations

We can't talk about cheating without examining our childhoods, questioning our family dynamics, revisiting traumas, facing our biggest fears, and reflecting on who we are and who we want to be. While it's not the most romantic of third-date conversations, we really ought to be paying active attention to a prospective lover's childhood dynamics—because it's highly likely those dynamics will appear in the partnership in time.

How was this prospective suitor raised? What values did their family uphold? What's the moral compass in their family of origin? Are there parents present, and how has their presence or absence impacted this person? What are their thoughts about who their family members are today? Do their values align with those of their family, or have they gone out on their own? How well do they set and enforce boundaries?

Perhaps this is why I've never been much of a dater—being asked questions that make us vulnerable and hold us accountable can feel invasive. The asker is being nosey and the askee is being interrogated. Still, don't we usually know by the third date if we want this one to stick around awhile? If we're comfortable concluding that we could fall in love with this person, why can't we be more open to real conversations about trauma? Specifically, how unchecked traumas still affect us. If we think we're ready to allow ourselves to fall in love with this person, why in the hell wouldn't we be brave enough to find out what kind of partner we're falling in love with? If marriage has evolved over the decades, shouldn't our approach to partnership follow suit? Shouldn't we be more emotionally available for tough conversations as early as possible in the courtship? Shouldn't we know whom we're starting a life with?

Here's a simple yet powerful example of how upbringings can impact a marital foundation. When I was growing up, our pantry was bare bones—there was minimal food to be found. My husband's was filled with an abundance of food, but he was scared to eat any of it because of a heavy-handed stepfather. I learned to be a creative cook in order to survive. He learned how to sneak around in order to survive. I had an empty pantry but all the love I could have asked for. My husband had a full pantry yet was forced to choose between going hungry or lying and stealing in his own home. My parents didn't have much to offer me financially, but I knew I was loved. My husband's childhood was filled with physical abuse at the hands of a man who couldn't show love. Needless to say, these weren't the things we were opening up to each other about on our third date.

Cheating isn't about body parts. Cheating is about unhealed traumas and unquestioned egos.

It's also important to understand that the physical act of infidelity isn't where the hurt resides. The debilitating trauma of infidelity is a result of every nerve touched leading up to the infidelity. Every missed dinner. Every night out with "friends." Every lunch you never knew about. Every pause when something didn't make sense. We aren't hurting because our partner's body parts touched another's—we're hurting because we didn't know our own lives. Infidelity is like a disease of the brain. It seeps into every memory, every experience, every moment of the life you were sharing with someone else. We aren't hurt because of the sex; we're hurt because of the façade our lives have become.

Paying attention to who the other person is and how they operate can't insulate you from being cheated on, but it can soften the blow (no pun intended). No number of third- or fifty-third-date conversations can prevent infidelity. Still, seeing the patterns in the life of someone we love and holding space for their blind spots can make trauma more manageable.

We are humans living human experiences—avoiding trauma isn't a realistic game plan. Taking it less personally, debunking our victimhood, and knowing that we can manage our feelings can make trauma less traumatic.

Back when we were living in caves, survival was straightforward. It was about food and food alone. Have food, live. Don't have food, die. Today, humans don't want to simply survive. We want to thrive, and this requires more emotional balance. Thriving involves taking control of your feelings while giving yourself the freedom to feel. Not an easy task, I know.

Today, the difference between surviving and thriving is found in our emotional stability. A marriage can support this stability or hinder it.

I wrote this book mainly to answer the question of how we heal ourselves. My gut tells me the answer is "pick yourself up and repeat." My experience tells me it's more complicated than that. I've been cheated on in many relationships. Maybe even all of them, now that I think about it. I can't help but wonder—if I'd taken the time to heal a bit more in the past, from my own traumas, would I have picked differently the next time around? If I'd been willing to heal from past hurts, would I have ended up living such a big one now?

Living a full human experience

I recently got hooked on the television series *The Good Place*.[3] If you haven't seen it, put this book down and watch every episode of the four seasons, and when you get to the last few, soak it all in and bawl your eyes out. This show has the power to change the world. The premise is centered around this question: What makes a full human experience? Without giving anything away, it involves ups and downs, yeses and nos, love and heartache, joy and sorrow. Of course, we logically know this to be true, but it can be easy to forget when experiences very nearly break us.

When it comes to healing, it's critical to remember we can feel more than one thing at a time. It's easy to believe we are either happy *or* sad, loving *or* angry, excited *or* hesitant, trusting *or* cautious. But you can be happy *and* sad. Loving *and* angry. Excited *and* hesitant. Trusting *and* cautious. One could even argue we're at our best when we're living in duality. Our souls long to feel many things in their time on earth.

Our time here on earth is exactly that—our time. We might feel we have no control over it, yet it's the only thing we're fully in charge of. Who we are during our time is completely in our hands. We come into the world alone, and we leave it just the same.

We can invest in ourselves enough to ensure we're at peace with ourselves, so we can be more present for the people we *choose* to love. We can choose to love fully aware that in doing so, we'll almost certainly be let down—because none of us knows how to live a perfect human existence. It's all part of the experience.

Love is a volatile commodity. We invest with the full understanding that there will be a crash at some point, whether large or small. Still, we can't just invest once and walk away. For love to become a strong asset, we have to invest regularly, in both ourselves and our partners. But we get to decide if our marriage is offering more than it takes.

In many parts of the world, marital values are being challenged. The ability to end a marriage is a relatively new phenomenon. At no other point in history have we been able to create a home on our own terms—though lord knows many still cannot.

We can enter a marriage with the intention of loving ourselves fearlessly. With the intention of investing in ourselves as much as we invest in our partners. Sometimes we *should* focus on only our needs. We should put ourselves first on our lists. We should be selfish enough to set boundaries. And we should be familiar enough with our needs to enforce these boundaries.

To live the full human experience, we need to be brave enough to ask the hard questions, even on the third date. We need to disengage a bit from the intoxication of new love so that we can fully see the person we're making a life-altering commitment to. We need to love ourselves so we aren't willing to overlook critical value differences simply because we want to be in love.

We can be in love with ourselves if being in love is all we're looking for.

Cheatin' on
the Mind

Dare me to say it? I'm gonna say it. At some point in every marriage, there's cheating on the mind—of either one person, both equally, or some percentage in between. Whether we admit it or not, for most of us, cheating isn't too far removed from our daily lives. It's a dark side of marriage that's difficult to admit to because we're so afraid that admitting it brings it to life, makes it a real possibility. But the truth is, cheating is always a real possibility in our marriages.

The institution of marriage came into existence approximately four thousand years ago, and even then, people weren't faithful.[4] Perhaps it's time to reexamine the idea of marriage.

Until only relatively recently, marriage was about the survival of the human species. Period. It was about combining forces, forging alliances, blending bloodlines. It served to keep our species at the top of the food chain. Over time, marriage became something with more choice involved. As choice grew, so did demands.

No longer is marriage about keeping us alive. Now, it's supposed to keep us alive while also fulfilling our minds and souls. Our spouse is supposed be our closest friend, the person who supports us through every challenge life throws at us, an equal partner in raising children, and in general, the person who helps us become our best selves. They're supposed to support our mental and emotional well-being, be our biggest cheerleaders no matter what, be our spiritual guides, our dream chasers, our stability makers, our [insert your most grandiose desires to be fulfilled by another human being]. They are expected to be our everything. That's a lot of pressure to put on any one human.

Cheating is, and has always been, everywhere we look. The only real change we've seen in history regarding infidelity in marriage is that now we villainize the cheater and pity the cheated. Infidelity was once looked upon as something men just did; marriage now demands truth and honesty. Cheating hasn't grown in popularity, just the judgment surrounding it. All of that to say we aren't dealing with anything new. Cheating has always existed and will continue to. If we can accept infidelity as a reality in our committed partnerships, we can begin to have real conversations about why. Rather than ignore a marital norm, why not peel back the layers and truly examine what leads to betrayal and deceit in marriage?

One of my favorite outlets is television and film. I have six half-written screenplays and can study the art of film for hours on end. The Academy Awards are my Super Bowl. As a child, I'd dream of the day I'd win an Oscar for Best Original Screenplay, and I've been writing my acceptance speech since I was eight years old. Following the blowup of my marriage and family, every time I turned on the television, I was inundated with plot lines centered around cheating, indiscretions, and characters living double lives. While I'm sure they always existed, I had no emotional attachment to them until I was facing the situation in reality. The ferocity with which this type of plot line dominates film and television is no accident. I challenge you to find one decent series that doesn't have some strand of infidelity running through its primary characters. Infidelity is a core component of the human experience.

You can't avoid the messaging, especially when you're actively managing the aftermath of an affair. Everywhere you look is a reminder of the hurt. One evening very shortly after the break, I snuggled up on the couch with one of my girls, popcorn in hand, all set to watch a funny rom-com. Said film took a drastic turn, resulting in an entire storyline centered around infidelity. My stepdaughter, bless her heart, finally cracked the silence, saying, "We don't have to watch this right now." I just laughed through my tears, and then we laughed together and finished the movie. Because what else can we do? We can't insulate our relationships from cheating by not talking about it. Like it or not, most of us are going to find ourselves on one end of it or the other. We can't allow one of the most common human experiences to debilitate us every time it's thrown in our face. Well, we can. Some do. I'm saying let's don't.

If we were to run and hide every time popular culture reminded us of the particular hurt we're facing at any given moment, we'd end up shutting out the world entirely. Does that mean those who've faced the death of a loved one can no longer be exposed to art about death? Of course not. That's the purpose of art—to help us feel the hard emotions and process them, and then to help us heal.

A prime contemporary example of infidelity is in *Sex and the City*, when Steve cheats on Miranda—one time, with one person.[5] He subsequently comes clean about it, recognizing the error of his ways, and begs for forgiveness, vowing to never betray her again. The storyline was written in such a way that the masses could conceivably forgive Steve for his wrongdoing. The way to do that? Minimize the impact, maximize the empathy. Poor Steve felt so disconnected from Miranda—what else was he supposed to do? Well, not stick his penis where it didn't belong, for starters. But that's just me.

When it happens in real life, the story is rarely so tidy. While adultery is entertaining on-screen, we aren't living in Shondaland. We're living here in the real world, where everything isn't so clearly justifiable, where the pain of betrayal can haunt us for years, where we don't always have an answer by the end of the season. We live in a world where forgiveness must happen daily, sometimes hourly.

Infidelity in real-life marriage isn't one lie, one time, with a full confession and absolute faith in the changes promised. Infidelity in real-life marriage involves a number of complex factors, including insecurities, unhealed trauma, and constant lies, either overt or by omission. Infidelity in real-life marriage isn't just about infidelity. It's about decades of learned behaviors oftentimes going back many generations. It's about how we learn about masculinity. It's about how we learn to love others. It's about whether we can face our truths. It's about how willing we are to be honest with ourselves and those around us. Infidelity in real-life marriage has almost nothing to do with the actual cheating and everything to do with choices we face on a daily basis.

Perhaps that's why infidelity can be found right under our noses, everywhere we look, served up on a pussy platter. We don't have to look hard—we don't even have to find it online. There are enough people unable to face themselves to ensure that cheating is always an option if we want it to be. Again, no amount of protective measures can insulate a relationship from infidelity. It can happen on any level, whenever someone wants it to happen. All it takes is a couple of souls willing to push aside the feelings of others in order to scratch an itch so that they don't have to face the hard truths in their own lives. The world is filled with people who would rather create drama than face their fears.

When the opportunity presents itself, we have to have the backbone, the morality, or the inner wisdom to turn it down. And I assure you, the opportunity will present itself. I place the blame squarely on the shoulders of the adulterer. The influence of the world didn't drive me to cheat on my partner, and I fully expected the same in return. That said, when taking into account the rampant subliminal messaging about what it means to be a man—to be highly sexualized, to lead with the penis—the fact that someone we love can find themselves so lost makes more sense. As a society, we've conjured up the myth that marriage is monogamous, yet we've mandated that masculinity be ever connected to sexual conquests. Unhappy marriages live in the dichotomy that tells us marriage should be one thing and masculinity should be another. The two cannot be mutually exclusive forever. Someone will end up getting hurt.

I'm using *masculinity* in a general sense, to refer to traits. Regardless of the sex assigned to us at birth, hiding emotions, compartmentalizing feelings, wanting others to want us, allowing ego to make decisions, believing personal value comes from sexual conquest—these are traits generally associated with masculinity. Does that mean women don't cheat? Absolutely not. Current research shows that women are almost as likely to cheat as men.[6] I'm not sure that's the equality our feminist foremothers had in mind for us, though.

Again, no matter what your marriage looks like, cheating will always be a possibility. I did everything I could to keep from being cheated on, and it wasn't enough. It did teach me some things, though. It taught me that my partner will never be everything for me, and that's okay. Most importantly, it taught me that I don't need to live for someone else to get love. I can love myself when I need love. I don't have to have all the same hobbies as my partner and go to all the same places and drink to keep up and wear the sexy outfits and give all the blow jobs and be the nanny and the maid. All these things still weren't enough. So now I take care of myself. First.

The Kids Are Not Alright

The infidelity in my marriage came to light on a Monday evening. My husband and I sat four kids down that Thursday to tell them we were separating. That experience was every horrible, awful thing you could imagine it to be—tears, anger, disbelief, even a broken hand. We had promised this family forever, and we were breaking that promise. We were breaking their hearts. We spoke with as much love as possible. We were as honest with them as possible. We explained that they'd go away to the beach for the weekend while I moved out. They were numb. We were ill.

I moved out on Saturday.

Deconstructing a family we'd spent over a decade creating . . . well, honestly, it was the hardest thing I've ever done. I worried about everything. Would my oldest son feel as if he'd lost the only father he'd ever known? Would my youngest child face a lifetime of back and forth between homes? Would my stepchildren feel I broke every promise I ever made? How would this change them forever? Would they be okay?

I left our home because it gave me some control in a situation where I felt as if I had none. I knew well enough that I couldn't heal inside the home that had broken me. I didn't know what healing meant in terms of my family, only that I'd come to a place of self-preservation. To maintain my stability, I needed to leave and set up a new home. So that's what I did.

For the first few weeks, while the three school-age kids were finishing the school year, we maintained the same schedule as much as possible. We picked up, dropped off, and shuttled. We let them lead when it came to what beds they wanted to sleep in and in what home they wanted to eat dinner. We drove out of our way on school nights if it meant they felt seen and heard. We didn't speak ill of each other. I know that sounds unbelievable, but it's the truth. At this point, I wasn't angry. I no longer had the energy to be angry. I was desperately hurt. I didn't want them to hate their dad, and I didn't want to hate him either. Moving out allowed me the space I needed to interact with him without hating him, so I was better able to help them love him.

When summer arrived, my stepchildren chose to live with their mother, my oldest could barely bring himself to visit my new home, and my husband and I continued taking care of our daughter from separate homes. The first few weekends I spent alone, I surrendered to the hurt. I didn't get out of bed, I rarely ate—I could barely move. Facing the idea of missing entire portions of my kids' lives was debilitating. That's when the anger set in again. I raged that I'd miss out because of someone else's actions. The infidelity I could heal from. Sharing my daughter turned out to be much more challenging.

While we tried our best to put our children's needs first, they saw us break a lot in the beginning. Me in my heartache, him in his shame. Still, once they realized there wasn't going to be hate between us, they started to feel steadier. They could manage us falling apart from time to time. What they couldn't have managed was us putting them in the middle of our hate. If I had led with anger and he had led without accountability, they wouldn't have been okay. It's not as if our family was exactly thriving in this time, but we led with love, and I will forever be proud of that.

We tried to share with them what we were learning ourselves. My husband explained to the boys how his warped version of what it meant to be a man had led to breaking the most important thing he had. He brought them on his journey of examining his masculinity as he learned to love himself. He talked about his abuse and how decades of stuffing down his emotions allowed him to become someone he didn't want to be. I told the children that it was okay to love their dad, and that they didn't have to choose between us. I assured them I still loved him and that love doesn't just go away when something like this happens. We also didn't make any promises. My husband and I didn't know what our marriage would look like in the future, but we accepted that we'd always be family.

Some of our efforts to continue to show each other love backfired, though. Much like the would-be leaders of their family, the kids were confused, scared, and in shock. They didn't understand why I let him come inside my house, why I invited him to stay for dinner. "Why are you not madder?" they'd ask me. Why was I not screaming and yelling and raging, as I often did when they hadn't finished their chores or they got low grades? I chose to be honest, explaining that I'd never been broken quite like this before, and that often, anger simply took up too much energy. I also explained to them that I'd set the boundaries I needed. I had walked away and created a new home, and because of that I could still show him love—as long as he could continue owning and examining his role in our hurt.

I thought about how my children might very well find themselves in this same situation someday, and I wanted them to know that it's okay to love people who hurt us, without letting them run over us emotionally. I wanted to show them how to walk away from a personal crisis being the person you want to be. I wanted them to know that we could feel nothing but anger for the rest of our lives, but that we didn't have to and it was our choice.

Some of the kids came around sooner than others. Some talked to my husband openly after a few weeks, some after a few months. Some came to it on their own, others needed more time and coaxing. I did some coaxing on my husband's behalf because I'd already learned that harboring anger hurts only you. Eventually, they started to believe that even if our family was changing, it could evolve without hate.

I'm glossing over many of the heart-wrenching details of that period, of course, because these are my children, and their feelings mean far more to me than any book. Perhaps they'll grow up and write their own books someday, but it's not my story to tell for them. Suffice to say, mending a family after heartbreak is horribly difficult, even with the best of intentions. It's not easy to look at someone who has hurt you and keep the rage at bay. But your children are watching. The better you do, the better off they will be.

Since my husband and I have reconciled, I now have different worries. I worry that the girls will think it's okay to be cheated on, or that they'll think I let someone mistreat me. I worry that they won't ever learn to trust in their own relationships. I worry that the boys will think it's okay to be unfaithful, to let the ego make decisions, to intentionally hurt the ones you love. I worry that they won't see the consequences of the actions, the growth required to move forward together. Then I remind myself that they're living this right along with us, often growing well beyond us. Their hurt and joy is just as significant as mine. We've all been changed, but how we allow the change to alter us as individuals is entirely a personal choice. As a family we've been fractured. The fracture will forever show up under x-ray, a permanent reminder of an old injury, but we can still heal and gain full mobility. Perhaps with the right regimen, we can even expect a full recovery.

Sharing hard truths

When I left our home after uncovering the infidelity, the well-being of my children outweighed my desire to carry and display hate for my husband. I chose to love him. That didn't mean I talked to him all the time. That didn't mean I could be around him often. That didn't mean my marriage wasn't ending. It meant I reassured my kids that I didn't hate him, that it was okay to love him. I reassured him that I'd loved him before, and I loved him after. I tried to explain that it was okay to have love for someone who has hurt you, and that it's okay to put boundaries in place. The concepts aren't mutually exclusive.

By depersonalizing a situation like this, you avoid being a victim in your own life. Because I wasn't a victim, I could teach our kids that they didn't have to take sides—they didn't need to stop loving him on my behalf, nor did they need to protect either of us. During our separation, my husband and I showed them that it hurts when relationships change, but that they can change without hate. Change can happen in a loving way. It *needs* to be done in a loving way, so that the next three generations don't suffer the fate of their great-great grandparents who broke up and couldn't stand to be around each other again, forever dividing a family.

I've tried to teach my kids that we can have happy moments while sad things are happening. We can laugh when our family is in crisis. We can even enjoy each other's company while we are angry and hurt. We're capable of experiencing more than one state of being in any given moment. Part of the wonder of being a human is that we can have feelings simultaneously. When bad things are happening, we can still be joyful, still make peace, still feel love. Sad things will happen, relationships will end, new ones will begin. The pain must be felt, but we don't have to take up permanent residence in heartache.

As I watch our four amazing offspring, I see how they're maturing into insightful and loving human beings. It's been a long road in our blended family, and it will likely get even harder before it gets easier. Still, I'm proud of us. The kids we've been assigned to in this life know how to love and how to forgive, both themselves and others.

How we talk to our kids when a marriage breaks matters so much more than the breaking itself. The decision to reboot a marriage shouldn't be rushed, even if it means immediate emotional relief for the children. We don't have to have answers—we just have to walk them through why we don't have answers for them yet. We have to help them understand that deciding the next best step for everyone's future is not a right-now kind of decision. It's a whose-home-will-you-bring-my-grandkids-to kind of decision. It alters the trajectory of an entire family. It will affect where the kids go to school, whom they'll meet, where they put down roots, how their lives take shape. If you've separated and don't have a final answer for your children, tell them that. Tell them it's an in-between phase. Tell them sometimes in life, when things don't go as planned, it's best to regroup so that you can make a solid next decision. Tell them you have a lot of the same questions they do.

I've raised kids over four decades of my life, from my teens to my forties. In every decade I've faced trauma and crisis. Still, in every decade I've become a better parent and mother. I keep learning. And I've learned that any number of factors should be considered when deciding what our kids need to know—and what they don't need to know. While it was mostly my decision to tell our kids *most* of the truth, my husband and I were both grateful we did. I knew firsthand how debilitating it can be to feel as if you don't know truths about your own life. I didn't want our kids to feel the same. I'd felt the sting of hiding and lying, and of the behaviors that make you doubt your sanity and question what you believe to be true. I didn't want our kids to feel the same. I'd known something was wrong and I kept blaming myself, thinking I could fix it if I just did the right things. I didn't want our kids to feel the same.

Children will often interpret a failing family as somehow their fault. To lessen the effect of that specific harmful belief, my husband and I were honest with them. We can show our kids how to forgive and heal and be loving, but it's much harder to convince them it's not their fault their family is breaking if they don't have a real reason for why their family is breaking. Our most important job as parents is to guide our kids in the least harmful way. I know our honesty with them caused them some harm, but it was the right decision for our family. I didn't want our kids to be afraid of facing hard truths in their own lives.

Dr. Ana Nogales explains it best in her book *Parents Who Cheat*: "While being told about a parent's 'bad' behavior is certainly upsetting, if it is done in a sensitive, age-appropriate manner, it is less harmful to a child than living with the doubts and confusion created by a parent's lies."[7] The afternoon my life imploded, I had an awful blowup with my stepson. I honestly don't even remember what it was about. I'm sure it was something along the lines of "take out the trash and clean up," then some talking back, then my correction at said talking back, then more talking back, then my harsher correction, and so on. Such is life with teenagers. My biggest fear was that he'd blame himself for the implosion. I was afraid that if we didn't tell our children the whole truth about why I was moving out of our home, some part of them would always wonder if they were to blame for any of it. They weren't. They were old enough to understand and old enough to deserve a real reason for what we were about to put them through. I also told them that we didn't have to carry shame about what our family was about to go through. I told them we would still love each other, and we would still love Dad.

Relationships change, living circumstances change, families change, but we can lead our kids through trauma and set an example of how to love each other unconditionally.

My husband and I could have avoided the real reason I was moving out of our home. We could have made up a PG-rated story about how our marriage just wasn't working out or how we needed space from each other or any other straight-up lie about what was happening to them. We could have done that, but I don't think it would have helped them as adults. If we hadn't been as honest as possible about the reality of what our family was facing, I would have remained angry and my husband likely wouldn't have felt any urgency to own his choices. I'm not suggesting it's appropriate to tell your children that "Daddy's fucking around and now Mommy has to move out." But our children didn't deserve to hear bullshit. They deserved to hear the truth (presented in the most thoughtful and loving way possible).

The bigger issue is how and why we tell them the truth. Is it digestible for their age? Are we just trying to throw the evil, cheating parent under the bus so our kids hate them too? Are we being overly honest to undermine their relationship with their other parent? Are we using honesty as a justification because we need our kids to be our support system through the hard times?

Or are we being as honest as their maturity level allows for? Are we answering their questions in a way that's kind and loving? Are we leading them through honesty while also teaching them they don't need to hate on our behalf? Are we being honest to help them, or to help ourselves?

When we lie to our children, they feel the same self-doubt and inner turmoil we feel when we're being lied to. We might believe we're protecting them, but we inadvertently communicate to our kids that we don't believe they're strong enough to handle the truth of what's happening to them in their own lives.

They are strong enough.

But lead with love.

Giving Our Fears
a Voice

S peaking your truth is harder than it seems, even for a loudmouth like me. To speak it, you have to be willing to face it. You have to be willing to examine what you're trying to hide.

When it comes to speaking truths, many of us are afraid, and we bury this fear under bravado, ego, selfishness, resentment, anger, and rage. But what if we didn't? What if we showed up for ourselves, maybe once a week in a counselor's office, and gave life to the fears we spend so much energy silencing?

What happened for me, when I decided to show up for myself in this way, is that I became less afraid. Okay, maybe that's a lie. Maybe I didn't become less afraid—maybe I simply stopped allowing fear to make choices on my behalf. I stopped allowing fear to hijack my mind so frequently. I stopped giving fear the power to influence the boundaries I'd set. I stopped overlooking the role fear was playing in my life.

Fear rarely manifests itself as fear. When we're afraid to love ourselves, it looks like hurting the ones we love. It looks like substance abuse to numb the voices inside our minds. It looks like reactive behaviors that scare our children, and combative conversations that destroy relationships. When we're afraid to see the dark parts of ourselves, those dark parts become us. They take hold in every crevice of our minds, and they lead every interaction we enter. When our fears go unchecked, unaddressed, and ignored, we start believing them.

We give life to every thought, emotion, and feeling that enters us. If we were giving life only to every positive thought we have about ourselves, or internalizing every loving emotion and feeling we come across . . . well, if you were doing that, you probably wouldn't be reading this book. Internalizing the good isn't what most of us are doing. Most of us are hearing the broken record inside our head telling us we aren't good enough, we aren't lovable, we don't really matter. And we're believing this bullshit. Then we're manifesting the fears created by the broken record in one of two ways: 1) Bleeding ourselves dry in an effort to convince the world and ourselves that we're good enough, or 2) Inviting the ego to compartmentalize our hearts and then hurting the ones we love because we don't believe we're worthy of love.

We humans typically internalize negative interactions at significantly higher rates than positive ones. It's by design, really. As humans, we grow via conscious thought. Our purpose is to progress. Progress tends to happen at more extreme levels when it's spurred by hardships. We stretch more when we experience infidelity, heartbreak, and the death of loved ones. We find sunsets, laughing babies, and puppy breath beautiful and inspiring, but these things typically don't force us to take stock of our lives and overhaul what's no longer working for us. Generally speaking, we take the beauty in our lives for granted and we're jolted into change when trauma is thrown at us. But change makes us uncomfortable, so we get stuck in fear of it.

Part of what many of us want in a marriage is for our partner to carry us through hard parts. That's an unrealistic expectation, even in an evolved, mutually respectful marriage. We must do the hard work for ourselves. Marriage can't do it for us. Marriage can, however, play a highly influential role in whether we feel free enough to do our own hard work. Marriage can either encourage or paralyze us. Marriage can give us the space and solid ground to continue working toward the version of ourselves we want to become, or it can hold us back, paralyzing us with the familiar. Can we speak our truths, to ourselves and to each other, or not? That's the defining difference. Perhaps the old adage "The truth shall set you free" is more applicable than we give it credit for.

Truth doesn't have to break a marriage. We can choose to speak our truths and make a conscious effort to be present for our partner when they speak theirs. If we hide from each other in our marriages, they'll eventually break anyway.

Stephanie Coontz reminds us of the fallacies through which we often view marriage in her book *The Way We Never Were*. "Within forty years, marriage changed more than the last 5,000,"[8] she writes. What we're expecting of marriage today is a hundredfold more than what any generation before us expected. Our life partners are now expected to be, well, perfect. Perfect for us, perfect for our kids, perfect for our finances—an all-around smorgasbord of perfection. Perhaps you didn't get the memo: no one is perfect. Where does one make time and space to personally evolve as a human and battle all their demons if the world is telling them they have to show up perfectly to have a happy marriage and family?

There are hard truths in the world. Truths that we need to face for ourselves, our families, and our extended families. "It's easier said than done" is another adage that's very true. Being unconditionally honest about who we are and how we came to be this person in this moment, in this life, is much easier said than done. If it were easy, everyone would do it, right?

Everyone doesn't do it—that's why it's not about love. Everyone doesn't take conscious action to feel, heal, and evolve through the hurts picked up over the years. Everyone doesn't take an honest look at how past abuses and prior traumas impact the choices we make in our current lives. Everyone doesn't acknowledge the unconscious patterns our minds create from surviving hardships. Everyone doesn't show up for themselves to say and feel the hard things that will allow them to love themselves more wholly. Everyone doesn't do these things. So we have to be very intentional about how and if a relationship works for our well-being and our soul's journey. We have to be honest with ourselves about how much of our well-being we're willing to sacrifice in order to alleviate a partner's burden. We have to be truthful about how much we can endure without it hindering us from who we want to become.

If you're looking for advice, here's all I've got: put yourself in whatever environment offers you the most peace, clarity, and self-love.

People can bamboozle us. Humans can say one thing and do another. The smartest of smart can be deceived and duped. Still, if we treat ourselves in loving ways, if we accept that hurt humans hurt others, if we choose grace every time we're capable, we can learn to love ourselves better. If we look at our own faults and pat them on the head in acknowledgment without hating any part of who we are, we can confidently love while also setting and enforcing the boundaries we need for our mental and emotional stability.

When we learn to love ourselves, we trust our choices, we better manage the feelings that lie to us, we more easily silence the asshole inside our head who tells us we aren't good enough, we accept people for what they have to give, and we enforce boundaries around what they try to take.

When we learn to love ourselves, we can more easily speak our truths.

Ten Easy Tips for Managing Life After Infidelity

I'm no expert. I'm not a psychologist; I'm not a counselor. I'm an author. I help the everyday life of one connect to the everyday life of all. I don't believe in telling people what to do with their lives. I do, however, believe in getting your money's worth. So to wrap up this section, I'm going to tell you what to do because you paid good money for this book and you probably expected someone to tell you what to do. Just remember that it's not my job to tell you how to proceed with your life in the midst of it falling to shambles.

Before we get to the tips, here's what I learn every single time life clobbers me upside the head with the exact thing I said I could never handle: You can handle it, and you do.

"I never want to have a kid." You end up with four. "I'm finally happy with myself and I want to be single." You meet your husband three months later. "I'd never take my husband back if he cheated." You're currently creating Marriage 2.0.

Know that life has a way of giving you what you didn't know you needed. More times than I care to remember, my words have come back to kick me in the ass. I vowed for years that divorce would be unavoidable after infidelity. I was the loudest voice in the group when the topic came up. Looking back, I can see that my self-righteous indignation probably (definitely) made me unapproachable. I should apologize for that. I imagine I came on too strong, too hard, and too judgy. Expressing this view made me feel insulated. If my spouse knew that cheating would mean the end of our marriage, if he were confident I'd leave him, then surely he'd never cheat. Then I'd never have to leave him. Look how that turned out.

All right, here are my tips for managing life after you've been cheated on, in no particular order.

DISCLAIMER: These things are not easy to do. Not one of them. They are challenging and will take daily focus and reminders. You will fail. Often, even. They aren't intended as professional advice, and you shouldn't listen to me (or anyone else) when deciding what to do with your life.

1. Lead with love, not hate. Yes, this is hard, but it's necessary to prevent six more generations of hate. Teach your kids how to love through it all. This means you must be the example.
2. Leave. Get away—with kids, without kids, for two days or six weeks. Stay with a relative, go see a best friend, rent an Airbnb, visit a sibling, take a road trip. Just go away. You need perspective, and you cannot get that near your partner.
3. Protect your energy. Hide, write, read, retreat. You are under no obligation to respond to anyone. Conserve your energy for you and the ones who need you. If something isn't peaceful and fulfilling, don't let it in.
4. Understand that another person's cheating has nothing to do with you.
5. Feel secure in the knowledge that your life wasn't the lie. The marriage and family wasn't the lie. Your real moments existed and aren't wiped away because someone else's journey hurt you.

Your life isn't diminished by hurtful choices made by a person who hasn't yet learned how to love themselves.

6. Own your own choices and timeline. You do not have to bend for anyone—not the cheater, not the kids, not the in-laws, not your own family or friends. The good ones stick around and see you through the hard times with love, trusting that you know what's best for your life. Because you do.

7. Remember that you know what's best for your life. You know it when you know it, and not a day before. Feel free to tell people to back the eff off when you feel pressured. This is your life.

8. Accept that if your partner cannot love themselves, you cannot move forward together in a romantic partnership. You can still have love for them, even loyalty. You may still be raising kids together, so the relationship won't necessarily end, but it will change. Welcome to the modern marriage, where we marry for choice over necessity. You may have to choose a different kind of relationship if your partner doesn't yet know how to show up for and love themselves.

9. Allow yourself to break open and break down. Painful things happen. You cannot avoid them. The only way to resolve hurt is to feel it. If you don't just go ahead and feel it, hurt can derail your life.

10. Love yourself. Love yourself fiercely. If you actually love yourself, it gets easier enforcing boundaries, showing love to the person who's hurt you and your children, and seeing a bigger meaning beyond yourself.

SECTION TWO

The Breakdown

You cannot save people. You can only love them.

–Anaïs Nin

Learning by Osmosis

M y fourth-grade teacher had a poster up in her room I'll never forget. It was a picture of Garfield the Cat with a pile of books tied to his head. The caption read "Learning by osmosis." The visual is forever imprinted in my mind because it made the concept so thoroughly clear. If only we could strap a pile of books to our head and magically gain the insight from all the hard work that went into creating those books. Clearly we cannot learn by osmosis—we must actually do the work of reading the books, feeling the feelings, changing the thought patterns, and on and on. We must do the work because none of the knowledge in the world is going to help us if we haven't experienced things for ourselves.

Just before I discovered my husband's infidelity, I'd begun research-ing how the narcissist and the empath frequently pair up (I was likely connecting to my soul, which knew what my mind did not). The book *Highly Sensitive Empaths and Narcissistic Abuse*, by J. Vandeweghe, immediately intrigued me.[9] I'd never heard about how empaths and narcissists sought each other out. As I researched, I started to understand why they find each other so frequently. The narcissistic personality wants to be understood, while the empathic personality wants to understand. Someone with narcissistic traits wants someone else to love them because they cannot love themselves. Someone with empathic traits knows how to love others and is often willing to do the emotional work for their loved ones because it distracts them from learning how to love themselves. Essentially, we have two personality types who don't know how to love themselves, so they seek each other out to convince themselves they're lovable.

When it comes to empaths and narcissists, there's a spectrum. Family of origin, circumstances, life stage, spiritual path—numerous factors can impact where someone falls on this spectrum, and it may change over the years. Some of us may never understand what it means to feel what another person is feeling, while others may never be able to stop themselves.

You might be more empathic if you feel utter horror at the idea of sitting at a bar for fear strangers will talk to you. You might be more narcissistic if you like the idea of sitting at a bar because strangers will talk to you. You might be more empathic if you feel it's your role in a relationship to figure out how to say something so that the other person hears it. You might be more narcissistic if you think it's the other person's fault you don't hear what they say. You might be more empathic if closeness and intimacy seem overwhelming. You might be more narcissistic if closeness and intimacy don't feel very close or intimate. You might be more empathic if people feel they can talk to you about themselves. You might be more narcissistic if you're annoyed by people who feel they can talk to you about their feelings.

To be empathetic is to feel *for* someone else and their circumstance. Empathy allows us to put ourselves in another's shoes. An empath, on the other hand, actually feels what the other person is feeling. There's an energy transference, if you will. An empath picks up another's hurt and puts it directly inside themselves. An empath doesn't care for someone else by relating to what they're feeling—an empath cares for someone else by actually feeling the feelings with them.

Consider whether you've ever felt drained after spending time with a certain person. When you leave an interaction emotionally zapped and physically done simply because you were around someone else's energy for a period, this is a good indicator that you're an empath. It may happen when a certain coworker walks into your personal space or when your partner is in an extra needy season of life. You may take on another person's energy and then wonder why your mind feels as if it's reached full capacity. You might also assume someone else's energy through your body and then wonder why you have a crick in your neck for the next year. You may even put someone else's pain into your heart and never be able to pinpoint why you're struggling to love yourself. The empath must learn how to set boundaries so that they can be better aware of what they're allowing themselves to take on from those around them. The ability can be tamed—balanced, even. But only if you recognize it when it's happening. We cannot heal what we do not see.

Setting boundaries with narcissists can be difficult. We may have to leave these people, let them fall—see what they'll do when they're required to pick themselves up. Some will, others will not. Either way, you must focus on you, your growth, your future. It isn't selfish, even though it will feel that way. It's just the discomfort of putting yourself first, so that you can be stronger and more whole for yourself and those around you. For those of us unfamiliar with this concept, this is called setting a healthy boundary.

The empath must decide how much of their energy they're willing to hold for the narcissist in their life, and then enforce boundaries accordingly. A healthy boundary might look like not responding to a text message, or it might look like not engaging when being manipulated. It's okay to shut down a line of communication when it isn't healthy for you. It's okay to stop taking the bait. At some point, we all must ask ourselves how many sacrifices we're willing to make to make someone else's life more comfortable.

Narcissists aren't evil. They're our family members, our friends, our partners, our parents. They are broken people who very much have a choice to make: grow or don't grow. Shit or get off the pot. You can still love the narcissist in your life—you just don't have to carry their weight on their behalf. Just because a current partnership cannot move forward doesn't mean the love instantaneously makes a mass exodus. The love still exists, and that's nothing to be ashamed of. It's okay to love someone while you set boundaries. In fact, it's mostly a prerequisite. If you didn't have love for them, then you probably wouldn't need to be so intentional with your boundaries.

Narcissists don't seek out empaths to prey on their empathetic gifts, though it can feel that way from the viewpoint of the empath. Narcissists seek out empaths because they believe they'll learn by osmosis. They believe they can learn how to love other people by being close to someone who can already love other people. But, as Garfield so generously taught us all those years ago, you must actually do your own work.

Narcissists want to be better at loving others, but they're invested mostly in their egos. When they see a quality they don't have, they want it, and they want it now—so they take it. There's a layer of self-ishness that allows someone to take something instead of earning it. When the narcissist takes the quality from their empath counterpart, they don't account for the fact that they never learned how to use it. So now they've got this bag of empath qualities while their partner is one bag short. Only the narcissist can't even use the stolen qualities, so they go to waste. Thus, the cycle continues.

In these narcissistic-empath partnerships, there is so much hope because the feelings are real. The narcissist genuinely wants to learn how to love and the empath believes they can help the narcissist grow into their full potential. The empath isn't being intentionally tricked and deceived. The narcissist has simply tricked and deceived themselves. The narcissist gets frightened by the realization that learning how to love isn't just about proximity. Then, to avoid the hard self-reflective work, the narcissist begins to drain the empath at higher levels, in hopes of not having to feel too much themselves. The empath begins to feel more and more unsteady, often questioning themselves and not knowing why. Once backed into a corner, the empath recognizes their power has been zapped, then distances to regenerate themselves. When the empath pulls back and quits giving so freely, the narcissist is forced to actually do the work or lose the ray of light they feel they so desperately need because they cannot be their own source of light. They do the work. For a little while. Until the cycle starts all over again.

A run-of-the-mill narcissist isn't preying on empaths to manipulate and destroy. The harder truth is that their loved ones are collateral damage. Their real target is themselves. They're seeking to destroy their own fears and insecurities, but their attacks often take out much more than that.

This is precisely why it's so hard for an empath to leave a narcissist. We believe in them. We even have reason to believe in them. What I finally came to understand, however, is that you cannot build a future based on what someone is going to be. Promises about who you'll be aren't enough for me anymore. To be in my life now, you have to already be who you say you are. I no longer live in future tense. Hope alone is no longer enough to make me believe in someone. If you say you want to be an honest and loyal human, then I'm gonna need you to demonstrate those behaviors regularly, present tense, real time, right now.

If both partners aren't starting the race in the same wave, one may never catch up. One may feel as if they're running their ass off, and the other may perpetually pace themselves so as not to get too far ahead because they know that if they take off, there won't be any way to fill the gap. The partners end up holding each other back instead of picking their own paces, unable to see the other's personal journey as theirs and theirs alone. They become so codependent, so entwined, that they mistake each other's experiences for their own.

It's easy to lose sight of the fact that we're meant to complete our own journeys, not anyone else's. Yes, even in marriage. Perhaps especially in marriage. It's easy to forget our wants and needs in a partnership, especially a passionate one. It's easy to fall in love with what someone could be, overlooking who they are right now.

Most of us don't learn until it's far too late that regardless of your current commitment level in a relationship, you could be in love with a whole new person a year from now. People who find love are a dime a dozen, but nothing is guaranteed. I don't mean to dismiss the uniqueness of romantic love. I simply mean that we tend to think of falling in love as this once-in-a-lifetime event when the truth is, we can fall in love any time, any place. People leave, people quit, people stray, people move on. Take it from someone who didn't see it coming—it can happen. Being married is a choice. A daily choice that has the potential to turn into forever. Forever isn't the guarantee.

We aren't responsible for the psyche of another person, and we must do the hard work for ourselves. With that in mind, maybe we could look at marriage this way: both partners are responsible for their own life journeys, but each has a sexy sidekick as a witness.

Housing Crisis

In the hottest housing market in history, my spouse and I struggled to sell our home. While everyone else in the world was entertaining twenty-seven offers over asking in seven minutes or less, we had one offer the first day our house was on the market—for significantly less than asking. Naturally we declined because so many better offers were surely coming our way. We had it appraised, staged, and painted. In short, we addressed every potential concern, and there wasn't a second offer in sight for months.

I couldn't help wondering if the energy of the home was delaying its sale. It makes sense really, given the shitshow my life had become. What did people feel when they walked in? Could they hear the sobs coming through the walls, see the hostility permeating the floors, taste the guilt moving from room to room? Could they feel the lonely nights spent on the couch, the devastation of a family broken, the shame of an empty home?

Our family home was supposed to be the forever house. It was a home I'd painstakingly painted, decorated, and Facebook-marketplace furnished over the course of years. With ample bedrooms and space, it was supposed to be the home my grandkids visited, where our children and their families would celebrate holidays. It was supposed to be our future, forever a landing space as our kids grew up and flew away. I moved out of that home rather suddenly, but letting go of it took time. Regardless of the market, my heart didn't want to let the house love again. Does anyone have any sage . . . ?

Walking away from a family home because of someone else's choice is a hard pill to swallow. That day isn't one that I'll ever forget—nor would I want to because that day made me stronger. I knew I couldn't live in the home that had held someone else's lies, carried someone else's shame. I knew I had to leave that home because he could not. He could physically, even financially, but not spiritually. I'd already been broken inside that home; he still had some breaking to do. I was walking away to hold on to my sanity; he still needed to cling to his. I'd already suffered the lonely nights; his were yet to come.

I never felt as if leaving was a mistake. Hard? God yes. But a mistake? Absolutely not. I felt as though I was choosing myself for perhaps the first time in years. I felt it was up to me to lead the family through the trauma, and I couldn't do that if I didn't have a space to fully feel and heal. My time in that home had run its course. I had to tell it thank you for the shelter it had provided, show gratitude for the love it held, and then get the fuck out before I could change my mind.

Moving day was torrential. I mean literally. A hurricane had landed three hours away, off the coast of Texas and brought with it flash flooding (no, the metaphor was not lost on me). The movers I'd scheduled and paid a deposit for canceled two hours after they were supposed to show up with all my moving materials, namely boxes. So, there I stood, during a flash flood, my clothing and kitchen needs lined up on the ground. No movers, no boxes, no backup plan. I had approximately twenty-four hours before my kids would return from their consolation-prize beach getaway and little to no hope of making a new home for them by the time they returned.

After I cried it out, I picked myself up and called a close friend with a truck. In one breath I said I was leaving my marriage and did she happen to have plans that day? She was there in an instant, no questions asked. Don't tell me there aren't angels here on earth. As she started loading up vehicles, I phoned for reinforcements. A realtor friend gave me the number of a teenager who helped some of her clients with moving. He showed up and brought a friend. The four of us moved everything that was mine out of my home that day. I'm talking everything, including a chicken coop, twelve chickens, two goats, a couple of dogs, and a guinea pig. I was careful not to clear out too much of the home itself. I didn't want the kids to come home to missing picture frames and empty rooms. It was still going to be their home, after all, even if it wasn't mine anymore.

By the next evening, I had beds together, closets organized, and decorations hung. We might have been a family in crisis, but our home wasn't going to show it. It would have been easy to give up, give in to the hopelessness. Standing on my front porch watching the flooding, it would have been easy to convince myself that this was a sign I wasn't supposed to leave. It would have been easy to believe that I didn't have to leave to heal. It would have been easy to tell myself the kids would be better off if I stayed. I'd be lying if I said I wasn't wondering if all those things were true. Still, something deep within was brave enough to speak louder than all the doubts. *If this isn't right, if my marriage isn't over, if there's still hope for my family, walking away today won't change any of that in the long run.* I needed to leave to heal. For me, there was no other choice.

My rental quickly became home. Sleeping alone got easier. Cleaning and cooking for fewer people wasn't exactly a punishment. There had been points in my marriage when I longed for a weekend getaway at an Airbnb, where I had to worry about only me. In some ways, I was living that now.

In most marriages, people hit a point where they don't know who they are anymore. It happens so innocently. We pick up the slack a little here, a little there. Before we know it, one person is picking up most of the slack. By the time we recognize what's happening, the habits of the marriage have been formed. The foundation solidified. Creating a new foundation can seem an impossible task. Sometimes we have to blow it up before we can rebuild. I'd blown it up—I just wasn't sure what I was building now.

The uncertainty is perhaps the hardest thing to deal with when a marriage snaps. Do we stay, do we go, do we try counseling, do we reconcile, do we divorce? It's anybody's guess what the next "right" step is. Our emotions lead us astray, our fears betray us, our hope blinds us. How do we know if we should stay or go, if we should fight through it or walk away? Unfortunately, I don't have those answers for you. I wish I did. I wish I could write up a ninety-nine-point inspection list, like they have for used cars, so you could just run down the list of what works and what doesn't.

What I *have* learned is that you must address your mental well-being before any other decision can be made. What that looks like is entirely up to you, but you must put on your own oxygen mask first. You must find a place in which you can process, feel, rage, and mourn while balancing daily life in the interim. We can be okay when our marriages crumble. It's a tall order, no doubt, but it can be done.

Everything Isn't Personal

Sometimes I have to remind myself that I don't need to take a stand on everything. I don't need to prove all the points, subtly or otherwise. I don't need to shun that family member just to show them how much they don't matter. I don't need to send that text message just to make myself feel better momentarily. I don't need to get in every dig that pops into my head. I don't need to insert myself into every situation.

Whenever I assume it's all about me, it probably isn't.

Life isn't being done to us. Even the awful-gut-wrenching-destructive-knock-you-on-your-ass kind of hurt doesn't have to feel personal forever. If we can make it less personal, if we can step outside ourselves for even a minute, we can remember that ultimately, we're only ever trying to learn how to love ourselves. Every other relationship is simply re-creating the opportunities in which we can learn to love ourselves.

So how do we depersonalize awful things (in this case, an affair) that have happened to us without compartmentalizing in the way that the loved one causing the trauma probably is?

First and foremost, we remember that we have the right to decide how we feel today. It took me decades to truly understand what that meant.

To be able to decide how I feel, I must give myself grace—every day, most days, some days. I don't always get it right. I must give myself the grace to show myself love when I don't feel it. Grace helps me intercept and neutralize the feelings I want to de-emphasize in any given moment. Grace helps me step back from my immediate feeling and remember my long-term goals. Grace helps pull me out of a thought spiral.

When I give myself grace, I can show love to others while also setting clear boundaries. Showing love doesn't necessarily mean regular contact or spending holidays together. Showing love can mean calling once a year or simply holding no ill will toward someone. Love can be limitless, but it doesn't have to be.

Second, we remember that infidelity is a major contributing factor in 88 percent of divorces.[10] If half of all marriages end in divorce and most of them are impacted by infidelity, it stands to reason that infidelity isn't a personal attack. Every person cheated on isn't doing something to cause the cheating, and every cheating person isn't just out to get laid by someone they aren't married to. Something more is happening here. Something isn't being talked about. Infidelity is a cultural norm lurking behind shame and secrecy.

Third (depending on where you are in your healing, this may sting a bit, but you need to hear it), we remember that it's just an affair. It's not that personal. The film *He's Just Not That Into You* allowed women everywhere to accept that someone not being into us isn't the insult we perceive it as.[11] In the same vein, neither is infidelity.

Depersonalizing how we got to where we are also depersonalizes the pain. With less pain comes less anger. With less anger comes more peace. With more peace comes more love. For you and those around you. Whether the marriage continues or dissolves after an affair, we must remember what Esther Perel teaches us in *The State of Affairs*: "Divorce is a reorganization."[12] Take the emotion out as quickly and as frequently as possible. Then retrain your brain to react to the emotional spirals less and less (more on retraining your brain shortly).

It can also be helpful to remember that the ending of a marriage doesn't equal failure. *Failure* implies it was all a mistake, that we shouldn't have done it or that we didn't get anything from it. When a marriage ends, it's an opportunity to rebuild a stronger foundation in our lives. We can change our lives. Change our circumstances. Change ourselves.

Choosing to not play the victim

In his book *Radical Forgiveness*, Colin Tipping defines victim consciousness as "the conviction that someone else has done something bad to you, and, as a direct result, they are responsible for the lack of peace and happiness in your life."[13] While trauma is personal, healing requires us to depersonalize it. If we walk around in victim consciousness forever, we won't ever love ourselves because we'll be too busy blaming everyone else for how our life turned out.

When someone hurts us, do we choose to become the victim because it makes someone else the bad guy? Can we walk away from infidelity without being the victim?

I don't mean to downplay the hurt. Trust me, I know the pain of being cheated on. Uncovering the affair in my marriage quite literally brought me to my knees. Many times, actually. But part of our rage comes from having chosen not to cheat while someone else did. We chose the harder path—setting boundaries and being honest—while our partner did not. When you find out someone has been unfaithful, it can feel as if you didn't get the memo about the rules in the relationship. It would have been a whole lot easier to give in to temptation along the path. You just thought you'd made a commitment not to do so. It's hard to keep your word sometimes, so when our life partners don't make that difficult choice, we can be left wondering why we ever did.

I'm not telling you to run out and cheat on your partner when the opportunity presents itself so that you don't feel as if you missed out on something just in case they are cheating on you. No, that would be wildly unhealthy behavior. I'm suggesting we depersonalize the hurt caused by infidelity. I'm suggesting we reframe how we look at infidelity so that we don't get trapped in victim mode. I'm suggesting we challenge the notion of victimhood by normalizing the frequency with which cheating in a relationship happens.

As humans, we can easily latch on to a persona that suits our current narrative. Someone cheated on us, we have been wronged, therefore we are the victim and cannot be held responsible for how we react. But if we all have the ability to cheat, and some of us act on this, can we really be all that surprised when it happens? We very often are, but why? What is it about cheating that surprises us? Is it simply that it actually happened to us? Is it that we were lied to? That our partner gave in while we didn't allow for such lines to be crossed?

To avoid getting stuck in a victim state of mind, we have to be real with ourselves. That's not to say we shouldn't move forward in a way that brings us peace, or that we shouldn't care, or that we should continue to allow ourselves to be hurt. I'm saying that cheating isn't the most surprising end to a relationship. It's pretty cliché, actually. If we can depersonalize the hurt, we can move forward in ways that don't impact us for decades. If we can see the action of cheating for what it really is—a relatively common human choice that stems from being out of touch with your soul—we can move forward in the life we have left without hate and rage and anger.

I used to think my marriage was my reward for all the hardships I'd faced before I met the one I promised my forever to. My reward after all the heartache and failed loves, after all the people who'd walked away from me, all the people who were supposed to show me unconditional love and could not. Turns out danger is always lurking and good people do bad things to the people they love. This is the way it is. We can learn to accept this with less judgment, less hatred, and more recognition of the fact that we're all humans going through life on individual paths.

It's natural to feel hurt and angry. I found myself wondering if I'd ever breathe the same again. Sometimes there's no way around the hurt. Sometimes it feels as if everything is a lie and we might never be ourselves again. Maybe we won't, but that's okay. Generations before us have managed infidelity, we will manage it, and future generations will manage it. The real question is how much we'll allow it to derail our journey.

It's tough to depersonalize our victimhood. Still, infidelity and betrayal are only ever about the person committing the acts.

Remember, we're only ever living our own lives.

I'll Take the Blame

It's possible to put someone through too many years of too much shit until, ultimately, they don't have a choice other than to choose themselves and walk away. I'm a little embarrassed to admit that every romantic relationship I've ever been in ended in my being pushed to the point of no longer being willing to be the punching bag.

Whenever I hit this threshold of unacceptable behaviors from partners, I'd vow to never find myself in the same place again. After the infidelity in my marriage, I took it a step further and vowed I'd heal and finally learn to love myself. I vowed to handle this intensely hard season better than I'd handled other intensely hard seasons.

"How am I going to do it better this time around?" I asked myself. "Having lived through trauma before, what am I going to do this time to come out better and stronger and more connected to myself?"

In *Think Like a Monk*, Jay Shetty introduces us to the differences between the "monkey mind" and the "monk mind." He writes, "Our minds can either elevate us or pull us down . . . the monkey mind switches aimlessly from thought to thought . . . without really solving anything." On the other hand, "We can elevate to the monk mindset by digging down to the root of what we want and creating actionable steps for growth."[14] Only a former monk could make it sound so easy.

When I found myself broken, I became laser focused on not letting my mind run wild. I'd force my monkey mind silent. I'd make space for creativity. I'd enjoy every minute I had with my children. I'd work out regularly . . . er, I'd try to work out regularly while holding space for myself and understanding that as my mind settled, my body would benefit from some physical flossing. I'm still working on that last one. I hate working out.

Regardless of how much inner work we're doing, when we hit our too-much-shit threshold, it may appear to the outside world as if we just snapped one day. Truth be told, we can be just as surprised by that snapping as the people who share our lives. A behavior that was acceptable for years might become the straw that broke the camel's back. Maybe it's a small slight. Maybe it's being called an ugly name. Maybe it's being told you're crazy. Regardless, we go down as the one who broke the relationship because we finally decided to enforce boundaries. We began to expect our partners to show up. Every single day. Just as we'd been doing for years.

In my experience, this kind of "snapping" happens mostly to women, and almost always once the children are older. When we emerge from years of unconscious caretaking of our children and partners, we're generally dumbfounded to realize how much of ourselves we've lost along the way. It generally follows years of begging for what we should have demanded from the beginning. Still, we're the ones breaking the contract. We're the ones who take the blame after pleading our case to have our needs met only to be brushed aside. It's okay. I'll take the blame.

I'm much less patient with my husband today than I was in our earlier years. This really should have happened the other way around. We should set higher expectations in the beginning of our marriages and then lower them as earned over the years. I didn't do it that way.

I believed that if you asked too much of anyone, they'd leave you. Best not set the bar too high. I accepted behaviors I should have left for. But I didn't. I didn't want to. I just wanted things to change. And change they did, over the years. Only I'd started with the bar so terribly below what I actually needed that I began to wonder if getting my needs met would ever be a possibility. That's not entirely my husband's fault. I was exceptionally angry at him nonetheless. I expected him to set my standards for his behaviors—at the exact level I wanted them set. Actual mind-reading shit. When he didn't, because he couldn't, I felt lonely and unseen.

I sacrificed my well-being when I shouldn't have. While I was busy losing my sense of self, my husband was living with relative freedom. His uncanny ability to compartmentalize meant that while I was at home falling apart, he was golfing. When our children were small, the thought of waking up on a Saturday morning and deciding what I wanted to do that day would have been fucking ludicrous. A mother of small children never wakes up on a weekend and decides how she'll spend even twenty minutes of her day. It's not her day; it doesn't belong to her. It belongs to every tedious detail it takes to raise four children, keep a full-time job, and manage a home. So when the children are finally old enough to fend for themselves, it takes a mother years to realize she's gained some of her personal freedoms back. The "mothermind" has become so ingrained that she doesn't even realize the chains have been cut. She stands in the prison cell long after the door has been unlocked.

Of course, being a wife and mother isn't a prison sentence. Mostly. It is hard, though, and to do it halfway well requires nearly every brain cell you've got. Over time, we forget who we are if we aren't someone's mother and someone else's wife.

I don't mean to generalize. I fully recognize the diversity of families. I also know firsthand how many mothers carry the emotional weight when it comes to parenting and marriage. I'm not saying other equations don't exist. I'm saying women often pay a high price to ensure their children and spouses have everything they need to flourish. And women are still primarily held accountable when things fall apart.

The emotional toll of family and marriage is a burden we don't often speak of. It's hard to say out loud that we feel as if we're drowning because we're generally judged when we do. Especially when our kids are young. We basically wake up every day and count down the hours until we can fall back into bed because everyone needs so much of us in those early years. Our kids (step, bio, or other) need us for survival, and our spouses need us to blaze the trail for them in parenthood and marriage.

The easy assumption is that women innately know what everyone needs at exactly the moment they need it. That's not true. From the sharing of our bodies to the sharing of our beds, we don't have any innate advantage making us more suited for the emotional weight of it all, even if the world tells us we should. We just offer ourselves up more freely to hold the burden. While the roles of marriage and parenting are evolving, make no mistake—mothers aren't getting to do less. We're still carrying the emotional load of our marriages and families. Maybe we do so because we know the perfectionism required to make everyone else's lives run smoothly, or maybe we simply fear that no one else will do it. Either way, we hold the burden. And the blame.

I remember looking around one day and feeling as if I were coming out of a twenty-two-year-long mommy coma. *WTF is happening here? I asked myself. Why is my husband so conditioned to think of himself first? Why do I feel unheard in my own home? Was I just the nanny and errand girl for the last decade? Why am I still dealing with loneliness and an often-drunk asshole of a husband? Why am I accepting less than what I want? Is that the level of compromise marriage requires? Can it not be more reciprocal? Can we ever be happy?*

It took me forty years to figure out it's okay to expect things from people. I watched my mom be independent her entire life. What that really meant was that she had no help from anyone, ever. I imagine what it would have been like for her if she'd had the support system she deserved—a partner, a parent, siblings, close friends, extended family. She had none of those when she was raising me. Her strength amazes me. My mother has grit. She gets shit done. It's amazing to have the power to be strong when you need to, but I wish she'd lived a life that didn't require her to be so independent. I wish she'd shared her life with people who gave back so that she didn't have to fight so hard to survive. I wish she didn't have to be so strong.

Affairs highlight the issues that already existed in a marriage. For example, it has come to my attention that I love anxiety, control, and bearing the cross whenever possible. Then getting really angry and resentful about it all when I reach max capacity emotionally and mentally. This has been my go-to pattern for most of my adult life. When my marriage broke and I walked away, I learned I could put myself first. I learned I didn't have to be everyone's everything. I learned that if I took a little time away from everyone else, I could give that time back to myself. I don't always have to come last. I took the blame for leaving my marriage but gained a relationship with myself. When my anger broke open, it no longer owned me the way it had for so many years. Most of my life, actually. Even most of my mother's life, and my grandmother's, and probably her mother's. Anger was a generational inheritance that I finally shed from my story, but it took breaking it open to learn how to do it.

Many years ago, while I was still raising my oldest on my own, I read *Burnt Toast*, by Teri Hatcher. The premise is that a wife and mother will give her loved ones the good toast and eat the burnt toast herself every damn time.[15] It resonated then and it still does now. We don't have to fill our family with the shitty pieces—we can just make another damn piece of toast for ourselves. We can take forty-five seconds to give ourselves something that isn't subpar by our own standards. We can matter to ourselves at least as much as everyone else matters to us. For too long, I didn't believe I offered value aside from fixing other people. I didn't know I offered value by just being me.

Esther Perel also explores the concept of accepting less than what you need in an episode of her podcast, *Where Should We Begin*. "Where did you learn to live on crumbs?" she asks a caller struggling to find balance and believe in her own needs.[16] What I've learned through it all is that we don't have to live afraid of needing too much, or worse, afraid of needing at all. Even if it means we take the blame for the final fall. Hell, we've been managing shit for years—it really doesn't matter who takes the blame—as long as change happens.

Remember, there are no failed marriages

A healthy reconciliation after infidelity (yes, it can be done), rather than one based on obligation or fear, requires the cheating party to lie down on their own sword. Reconstructing the marriage requires the human who has betrayed another to *not only* own up, *not only* fully accept the hurt created by their deceitful choices, *not only* feel the hard feelings, but also learn to love themselves so that they can better love the people in their life. This isn't a small order. Especially when they're coming from a place in which they're so disconnected from themselves that they've just dragged all their loved ones through the mud with them. Reconnecting to your soul after being disconnected from it, sometimes for an entire lifetime, is scary and deserves credit.

The flip side is that the betrayed person must grow a backbone and make choices for their own mental and emotional well-being, regardless of what the other half of the equation may or may not do for themselves and their relationships. At some point, one must reach a level of acceptance for the other person's journey. This doesn't mean excusing their actions. The betrayed must be honest with themselves as to whether moving forward in the relationship allows for their own healing to take place. Allows them to maintain their inner peace. Because remember, it's not about whether we love someone else. It's about how well we love ourselves. The backbone must stand strong. We must own what the soul can and cannot come back from. There is no wrong answer here, but your answer must be honest.

One partner may be able to take the necessary steps and the other may not. I'm going to go out on a limb and suggest that if both parties aren't actively participating in creating change, a marriage 2.0 may not be in the cards. Your marriage may be over after infidelity. That's the truth of it. For others, it may not be over but should be. Fear, a sense of obligation, finances—these aren't reason enough to stay in a life in which our souls can't grow.

Let's normalize the trauma of infidelity and accept that for some marriages, reconciliation won't mean a marriage 2.0. Reconciliation can mean feeling through the hurt, so that we can remember why we loved someone whose actions have caused us harm, and then creating a new life. It can mean reconstructing the family, not the marriage. To do that well is every bit as admirable. Just because a marriage ends, it has not failed. Either way, you're creating a new life. Either way, there's no shame.

We don't have to be in lives that no longer suit us, and we don't have to let the fact that the family changed define us forever. A partner may change and grow as desired, and you might still never be able to look at them the same again. You might be fully capable of healing alongside your partner, but they might not be as invested. You might both accept that the infidelity is a symptom of a much-larger disease inside your marriage and know that you're better off venturing into separate lives. All these options are perfectly acceptable.

Your marriage didn't fail, you didn't fail, and maybe you didn't even fail each other. Maybe it was part of our soul's journey and the right outcome is whatever the outcome is. Accepting this is part of loving yourself fully.

Maybe there doesn't have to be blame at all.

Journal Entries BC

(Before Discovery of Cheating)

The following are journal entries resurrected in moments of trying to figure out my marriage. Where did it go wrong? When did it begin to fail? How did we end up here? The entries have been tweaked only slightly, for readability. While they're raw, I know that so many marriages face similar ups and downs. My intention in sharing these is that we learn to reserve judgment for ourselves and for each other—because marriage is not for the faint of heart.

One Hundred and Twenty-Two Months BC

A year from now, I want to remember his smile as we sat outside for six hours, occasionally rotating our chairs to match the sun's rotation, completely content just to be next to each other. I want to remember the feeling of love in the most simplistic day. I want one million more of these days to follow and I want to remember to appreciate every single one of them.

Seventeen Months BC

He's off again. On his phone at odd hours, lots of middle of the night "shits," in general pulling away from me. I tell myself all the things I know to be true, but my mind remembers all the other things I know to be true. He's stressed out about work, his kids. He's not as sexual with me. I know now that when he disappears emotionally, he goes to dark places. I keep believing he should be past all of that now.

Fifteen Months BC

I want a divorce. It feels knee-jerk, and I may not feel this way in seventy-two hours because that's the ugly, beautiful truth of our marriage. But tonight, I want a divorce. I don't know if my marriage is falling apart or if we are just in a bad "season," as they say. I know we wake angry at each other at least as often as we don't. I know we frequently go to bed angry. I know when we talk about it, things get worse, and when we don't, they stay the same. Can a marriage become too damaged to save? His fix is to give it however many days it takes for the fight to be forgotten, then business as usual. That works until the next fight, then the cycle starts all over again.

Twelve Months BC

My marriage isn't consistent. The temperature swings daily and I never know what the state of it is going to be. We flow from days of actual bliss, happy, connected, taking on the world together, to nights on the couch, drunken fights, and cruel words. I don't want to be emotionally uprooted anymore. I want to roll over every morning and know there's a hug waiting for me, not roll over every morning to test the temperature for the day. Why always the up and down? Why "I love you to the end of the earth" followed by weeks of avoiding eye contact with each other? The workload of our marriage is unequal. I'm in counseling right now and I'm trying to figure out if people can only treat you the way you let them. Is that true? Have I allowed myself to be taken for granted? Do I even appreciate *myself* anymore?

Five Months BC

I'm hurting today. I've lost a significant amount of my mind energy. I'm fighting with my husband, or else he's fighting with me—and I can't care anymore. We do this a lot. It feels like we fight too much. Alcohol isn't helping. Our fights frequently last days. They used to last months, so maybe that's progress. The question is just how much is too much. At what point does the scale tip in one direction or the other? How much of a ratio are we looking for exactly? How frequently should we expect to feel bad? Some say never, others say it's part of the deal. I don't expect perfection, although I'm sure my family would tell you otherwise. I can accept conflict. Perhaps that's the problem—maybe it's not normal to allow conflict in your life so freely. I grew up in conflict. It's all I really know. Maybe that's not a norm for most people. Still, I don't need perfection. I can embrace the imperfection, but does disrespect have to be part of the deal?

I know I'm a recovering perfectionist. I know I said I didn't expect perfection in my marriage, and that part is true. But I expect perfection from myself, and it ends up rubbing off on everyone around me. I'm trying to learn how to forgive myself for my imperfections. It sounds stupid, "Learning to forgive myself for my imperfections." Like WTF does that mean. But I think it means accepting our questionable choices, embracing our unlikely paths, being okay with not doing the exact right thing in every single moment. A recovering perfectionist, I must also cut myself some slack, honor everything I do in a day, get comfortable around my inner fears. I'm making progress with managing the anxiety. I still get anxiety-induced shortness of breath, my mind still races at warp speeds, I worry about everyone all the time. I get migraines a few times a year, when the anxiety gets particularly harsh.

So when I've been fighting with my husband for days, when we visit this level of awfulness, it's everything I can do to not fall apart. Only there's always anywhere from one to four children within earshot. I don't get to have meltdowns, or if I do, I scare the ones I love most. I feel alone in my marriage. Sometimes I have no idea where he is, or when he'll be home. Other times I know damn well not to expect him because he's been golfing since 2:00 p.m. and it's now Friday night. He just does whatever he wants.

It's bizarre to imagine myself just waking up on a Saturday morning and making plans for myself. Just me, no one else, no need to consider my husband or my children. He won't feel bad, or come home early out of guilt, or worry about what's going on at home. Do all men compartmentalize this well? He can leave for a golf game while his wife falls apart in their bedroom. Wouldn't it be nice to someday meet someone who wouldn't be okay knowing I wasn't? Who put my feelings first? I don't feel like I've always been a priority in our home. It's like as long as I don't need too much, then everything is okay. I've recreated my childhood within my marriage. I wonder what a marriage without such deep cuts goes through. I wonder if there are marriages that don't endure so much hard shit. Is there a marriage where people mostly (or even always) see and hear each other? Where they give each other what they need? Is there a place in marriage where the hurts are healed, the wounds less visible, the scabs not so easily torn off? How do we truly heal a marriage without sacrificing too much of ourselves?

When we're so separated from each other, my gut wrenches with fear that his ego will seek the adoration it so desperately craves from someone who isn't me.

As I sit home with our collective children, I wonder if other wives also don't care if their husbands come home. Are they a little relieved to not have to handle him for an evening? I get that. If we don't have plans as a family, he believes himself to be free for the day. I know I won't have that kind of freedom until our kids are grown. But someday, I'll finally be able to wake up on a Saturday and think only about myself.

Four Months BC

I'm working on a freelance article about hindsight in 2020, and I'm wondering if I have any. How can we have hindsight in 2020 when we're still very much in the trenches? What hindsight is available if we can't yet look back? Hindsight assumes one has experienced, processed, reflected, and grown from something. If hindsight is a lifelong process, then how do we ever feel healed from our past?

One Month BC

A large part of our sex life is simply about keeping my husband satisfied because I've asked him to do me this huge favor of only having sex with me for the rest of his life. Sex goes from being something for us to just another "caretaking" chore on the list for the day. Feed and water dogs, stock up on groceries, make sure husband comes. I don't feel like I can say any of this out loud because it feels like it would just cause more arguing. It feels like I can't go changing the rules now, only this isn't really what I'd bargained for in the beginning. I used to feel like I was an integral part of our sex life. I used to want to pounce on him when he walked into the room. How does a spouse go from can't-get-enough to checked-off-the-list? More importantly, how do you go back?

Ten Days BC

I feel like I'm on the verge of cracking the code in my marriage. I'm seeing the picture of what our marriage is, the good with the bad. Our good parts are gifts, our dark parts are manageable. We have passion, we love working with each other, and we genuinely enjoy each other's company. We also have a lot of insecurities that get in the way of our peace. I'm realizing my ability to trust is more broken than I've been willing to admit. I often doubt things he tells me. It sometimes feels impossible to know what's real and what's my anxiety.

Journal Entries AD

(After Discovery)

Three Days AD

What do you wear when you're about to break four hearts? What will they remember of those moments when their world fell apart? Will they remember the wall colors we picked together, or the messy bun my hair was in, or the dogs piled up on the couch they were never allowed on? Will they feel immediate sadness, anger, shock? Will my son have a dad in ten years, his children a granddad?

How am I to still parent my husband's children when I no longer have a claim to them? God, why couldn't he have asked for help. Called a counselor. Acted to protect our home instead of hurting it. Devastating it.

Four Days AD

Three nights in a hotel and just like that, I don't live here anymore. I accidentally wrote *love* and had to correct it but that seems more appropriate, actually. It's funny the things you don't care about when you're about to pull the rug out from under your children—the grades, the chores, the dishes. The things I cared about so much just a few days ago really don't matter anymore. The backpacks on the floor, the cups lying around half full, the snack wrappers on the counter. None of it seems very important by tonight's standards. In twenty minutes, I'll ruin all their lives anyway.

Six Days AD

I'm sitting in a misplaced chair, listening to the rain, waiting for movers to arrive. I cannot believe this is what I'm doing today. I float between "I can't believe he did this" to "I'm so grateful I know so I don't fall for the trap of feeling like I'm crazy again." Still, how did my life become such a fucking cliché? I wonder if I should take my daughter's back-pack. Will I be ready for her by tomorrow at 5:00 p.m.? Can I make a new home for us in thirty-six hours? Should I let her have one home for one more night?

Eighteen Days AD

I want to be happy that he's starting all the projects around the house we talked about for years. Still, it hurts immensely. Now that I don't live there, he's happy to stay home and work on the house instead of playing golf every weekend. Now that I'm gone, he's happy to be home. I guess I should have left a long time ago. I didn't realize I was the reason he didn't want to do the things we always talked about.

Twenty-One Days AD

I'm tempted to do bad things. Text her. Guilt-trip him. Berate them both. Tell him how I feel at this moment right now. I tried to get dressed and leave the house today. I drove around for a while but couldn't commit to anything, so I cried in a parking lot then came home and got back into bed. I feel like I've lost my entire life and I don't know what to do. I'm just sick.

Thirty-Three Days AD

I just got seriously terrified that my new neighbors were driving over to introduce themselves. The idea of engaging with another human being feels impossible right now. Turns out they were just turning around, thank fucking god. I cannot people right now.

Forty-Five Days AD

I've been competing for my own husband, but I didn't get the memo. I want him to compete now. Like we're on a new season of the *Bachelorette*, only the surprise guest is the estranged husband who comes to see if the bachelorette will choose him again.

Only I'd be a terrible *Bachelorette* candidate because I'm not into hookups and I'm not into leading anyone on. It's inhumane to treat someone as I've been treated. Leading someone on, I mean. Feeding them lies to feed your own ego. That's just not who I want to be.

Fifty-Seven Days AD

I never understood the highs and lows of our marriage. I almost killed myself trying to understand them, manage them, and prevent them. For the first half of our marriage, I thought it was my fault. If I could just say it right. Do it right. Take it the right way. As the fog of personal blame is lifting, I realize that my husband has been battling some demons I knew nothing about.

Sixty-Two Days AD

I spent much of today setting boundaries with my daughter while she was with her dad, my now-estranged husband. "Ask Dad," I kept replying to her text messages. "Dad can answer any question I can," I keep reminding her. It's taking some time and a lot of not giving in to the mean things I feel justified to say, but I know it will eventually make transitions easier.

Seventy-Five Days AD

Was it my predictability? Did my faithfulness leave him bored? Just because I wasn't bored in the marriage doesn't mean he wasn't. Maybe I'm just not exciting enough of a person for him to be happy.

I guess what I really want is some chemistry. Someone to be invested in my well-being. Care and concern always. I want to share my life with someone, to have and to hold. To respect me and be loyal. Does that even exist?

I spent an hour making a playlist and then didn't feel like listening to any one of those songs. That's the place I'm in. I don't even know who I am anymore.

Ninety-Seven Days AD

Tonight I sat in my previous living room, on my previous couch, while my still-estranged husband did all the cooking and cleaning. I didn't lift a finger to pick up clothes or wipe down a countertop or fill a toilet paper roll. I have never sat on that couch while someone else did all the planning and cooking and cleaning. I don't have to because it's not my house anymore.

One Hundred and Seventeen Days AD

I don't want him to suffer; I want him to heal. I don't want him to pay for anything; I want him to love himself. I don't want to punish him; I want to unveil him. Who is this man I married a decade ago? Who is he when I'm not around? I want to see the missing pieces of my life. I want to know the parts of my life that were kept from me. I want him, but I want to enforce boundaries even more. I'm in a place where I can accept the end of my marriage. I'm in a place where I can accept that my marriage is over. *That* marriage is over, and it will never suit me again. I'm momentarily on hold in order to regain my inner calm and self-trust. Then I can see if this man can give me a different marriage altogether.

Laying a New Foundation

If I'm being honest with myself, my marriage didn't break because of an affair. The cheating was just the final blow that shattered the already broken glass. I was no stranger to being unhappy. My marriage was no stranger to dark periods, which were followed by weeks, sometimes months, of easy living. The time frames ranged, but the cycles were predictable. Life changes, stresses, insecurities, sickness—when our worlds shifted, so did our marriage. Ups and downs lurked around most corners. It's hard to grow when stability seems unreliable.

The oscillating between peace and conflict eventually took its toll. Drinking took its toll. Unkind words took their toll. Lack of respect took its toll. Still, had I not been cheated on, I would have continued accepting subpar behaviors in my marriage. I would have continued convincing myself that the good outweighed the hard, that it was just a phase we were in, that we could both get better. I could work on my anger; he could compartmentalize less. I could manage my reactions in a kinder way; he could be less closed off emotionally. I could have fewer expectations; he could have more. I could. He could. We could. But we didn't.

I would have loved it if he'd come home one day and said, "This marriage could be better, and I want to change to make it better." That didn't happen. It took me actually, truly, fully leaving for that to happen. I kind of wish I'd done it sooner, honestly. I thought about it so many times over the years. Then we'd feel better for a while and I'd believe we were actually, truly, fully getting better. And then, and then, and then. The cycle would continue.

What kept me in the marriage was our kids. I know that's not what we feminists are supposed to say. I know I'm supposed to say that you can't save a marriage for the kids, and that if you're happy, they'll be happy, and that no one deserves an unhappy marriage. I know those are more acceptable phrases, but sometimes I stayed because of the kids. If I was going to break their hearts, uproot their already previously uprooted lives, and further break wounds that were still mending, I'd better make damn sure it was fucking worth it.

Over the years, whenever I contemplated leaving my marriage, I wondered what we'd say to the kids. "Dad and I don't really hear each other, and we often feel disconnected." Or, "We don't seem to have the same marital values, and we aren't giving each other the freedom to grow into the people we want to be." Or, "Sorry, kids, Mom and Dad are going to tear apart your future because we need to go find ourselves." Shut the fuck up. Seriously. The hurt it would cause them to leave never seemed comparable to the hurt I was going through by staying.

These are of course very real issues in a marriage. In fact, the idea that you and your partner should be supporting each other in your personal and spiritual growth is kind of the point of this whole book. Still, to say it to your children as an explanation for what you're about to put them through? Well, a lot of us struggle with whether we're "justified" in leaving a marriage. For me, being unfulfilled in my life never legitimized my choice enough to walk away. So, we worked it out. Kinda. Good enough.

Then the cheating.

Once I had a "real" and "good enough" reason to leave, I did. Except the trauma that resulted from my leaving after the infidelity was likely much worse than it would have been if my husband and I had just sat our kids down earlier and told them our marriage wasn't working and we weren't setting the right example for them and that it was okay to expect more for yourself. We didn't. We let that train gain speed and crash hard, taking out four precious passengers along the way.

That said, had we called time of death on our marriage before the cheating, I would have always wondered if I'd done the right thing. I might have always carried shame, might have always believed that I could have done better, made changes, worked it out somehow. I might have always feared that I left for "no good reason." I'm not suggesting I should have put this pressure on myself. I just know I would have. The heartbreaking event offered a significantly easier escape route. And even then, I had to push myself very hard to physically move out of my own home. But once I did, I could breathe better than I had in years. Quite literally.

For years I had shortness of breath that would come and go, seemingly with no rhyme or reason. Eventually, it was impacting my health to the point where I went to the doctor certain I had lung cancer. I was hooked up to machines and x-rayed. Turns out I had anxiety. It had never occurred to me that my chronic shortness of breath was a direct result of the ups and downs in my marriage. I was given prescriptions for Xanax and sleeping pills and sent on my merry way. Needless to say, pills weren't the fix for what was wrong with me.

The pain of having left my home and marriage was debilitating at times, the loneliness palpable, the heartache real. But coming home to myself every day, with no one else's emotional needs dictating how

I felt or triggering my anger-filled responses—that was the fix.

I missed my best friend. I missed all the stupid little things we talked about on any given day. I missed the partnership. I missed him. But I didn't miss our marriage. I no longer wanted the ups and downs, the nights on the couch, the knots in my stomach. I'd *never* wanted any of those things. I'd simply started to accept them. I was too afraid to change the status quo. Until I walked away.

When we resurrected our marriage, the primary conversation was about how to lay down a different foundation. This time, it wasn't about love. It wasn't about taking care of the kids. It wasn't about dividing up household responsibilities—although all these things did need an overhaul as well. It was about creating a framework that accounted for what we both wanted marriage to look like. Hell, just taking the time to be honest with each other about what we both wanted and needed was something we'd never done before. Not loudly and boldly anyway.

While all the logistics of raising a family—who does what, who disciplines whom, who shows up when—needed to be addressed, the answers to these questions would be found in the foundational structure. If Marriage 2.0 was based on respect, openness, and acceptance, then we could talk about who would do what, how to effectively parent, and how to balance household responsibilities while feeling seen and heard.

Every time anything seems remotely similar to the old marriage, I become terrified that I've backed myself into the same corner—again. This is my current challenge. My mind can spiral quickly. My reactions are swift and strong when behaviors seem all too familiar. A sarcastic tone, a facial expression, or a perceived slight can send me into defense mode immediately. What I've come to appreciate is that my fear-driven response team would be appearing on the scene even if

I'd moved on to another relationship. Once bitten, one flinches. Had my husband and I not reconciled, I would have eventually entered another committed partnership. I suspect I would have flinched if that person had done anything to trigger the same feelings. The fear is a direct result of never wanting to feel lost in my own marriage again.

Regardless of the relationships we ended up in, a better foundation needed to be laid.

My goal will never again be to change someone, or tell them what kind of person they should be, or guide them toward the person they tell me they want to be. I've had to learn how to choose a person who can comfortably be the things I need without them becoming someone they're not. I won't ever try to rescue someone from themselves again—not my husband or anyone else. I'll never live only "our" life again. Which, I must point out, is significantly easier to do when children are older and less dependent.

Today, both parties are present in the marriage every single day. We hear each other, we don't run away from each other's feelings, we follow through, and we show respect through our actions instead of our intentions. I let my husband be his own person and he lets me be my own person, flaws and all. We no longer allow these flaws to be excuses for hurtful choices. We stand up for each other whenever possible. We lead with gratitude instead of insecurities. We're inspired by each other's successes instead of threatened.

As is the case in most marriages, what we have has always been beautiful. Our spark is real and bright. We've built a life together and supported each other through hardships. We've challenged each other and pushed each other to become better and stronger, all while raising four children to the best of our abilities and while running a company together. Importantly, though, I don't feel as if my entire identity is tied up in one relationship. I now know that should it all fall apart tomorrow, I'll be okay in time. We both will be.

We can still have love for each other, we can still parent together, we can still check our emotions and take a little pressure off each other. We don't have to be each other's everything. And if our marriage ends, it hasn't failed. It's an opportunity to build a new foundation.

Mending the cracks beyond the infidelity

Gambling, substance abuse, and pornography[17] often play large roles in cracking the foundation of a marriage. Before the cheating came to light, drinking was a daily priority for my husband and me. If we wanted to have fun together, we drank. If we went on a date, we drank. If we cooked at home, we drank. If we went out to lunch, we drank. We drank for different reasons—he to hide from himself and I to keep up. Drinking can take down a marriage. It can destroy families over generations.

Stereotypes about alcoholism can allow us to disconnect from the role alcohol is really playing in our marriages. If our husbands aren't stumbling through the door looking for a fight, and we aren't the stay-at-home parent secretly drunk by 2:00 p.m., then we're good, right?

No. Alcohol takes hold inside a marriage much more subtly. A few beers at lunch, a couple of glasses of wine at dinner, a whiskey or two as the night goes on. Marriages that share the stage with alcohol don't allow space for partners to open up to each other and be present with each other. The haze of alcohol can stifle a home.

In *Talking to Strangers*, Malcolm Gladwell explains that alcohol is no longer viewed as a mood enhancer—a substance that lifts the filters so we can say how we really feel. Instead, alcohol allows us to believe something completely different from what we know to be true in a sober state. Gladwell discusses research indicating that when we have nasty fights with our spouses after drinking too much, spewing words we'd never say sober, we're not speaking our truth. We're speaking lies. Gladwell explains that when we use alcohol, a "neurological burglar is turned on. We become altered versions of ourselves."[18] It changes us. It doesn't enhance us. It doesn't allow us to be ourselves. Instead, it makes us someone we're not. It allows for excuses in a marriage. It keeps two partners from being present with each other, sometimes daily. If we're rarely fully present, there won't be much of a marriage or family left to salvage.

Drinking in a marriage is a recipe for sadness and loneliness. It often results in one person doing much more of the work because the other one can't. Drinking breeds resentment, betrayal, and often anger.

If you and your partner can have a few drinks and enjoy each other, I'm not talking to you. Drinkers, real drinkers, are my targets right now. You can easily spot a drinker because they offer a lowball estimate when asked how many drinks they've had. They also believe you can't tell they've been drinking. I was raised by a drinker, I've been a drinker at points in my life, I married a drinker. I'm up-front and personal when it comes to the impacts of alcohol on marriages and families.

It starts out innocently enough, a nice summer day, some drinks on the patio. Then some more at dinner. Then a couple after dinner. Then chaos. Soon enough, we aren't dealing with the same people we were eight hours earlier. By morning shame has set in, by lunch, compartmentalization. When dinner rolls around, the best way to settle our nerves is to have a few more. Alcohol is not a friend of most marriages.

Creating change, mending the cracks, starts with intentionality. We must do something that moves us closer to healing every single day, sometimes multiple times a day, and recognize that we're doing it in the moment. Say you wanted to drink more water every day. How would you go about it? Sticky notes? Phone reminders? Preparation? If you don't remember to do something throughout the day, it likely won't get done. Intentionality must become a permanent fixture in your life. Change doesn't come from a few weeks of effort followed by burnout. Rewiring, or retraining, your brain takes minimal effort (this has been proven!)[19] but it must be done every day. The days you don't give growth one minute of thought are the days you don't move forward.

That's not to say we don't require rest and breaks. Cut yourself some slack when you don't finish a book about trauma while you're still living it. It's also easy to become a mindset junkie riding the high of self-serving growth. It's easy to start believing that your growth is superior to others' growth. Maybe it feels good to have faced enough of your demons to grow exponentially. But there's always a next level. I'm not fully healed; neither is my husband. We also aren't the same people we were two years ago. I don't think full recovery is ever the goal after trauma. Mostly because we aren't ever the same after trauma. Just days after our separation I said to my husband, "We won't be the same people in one year." I didn't know what that would look like at the time. I just knew this was a defining moment that would fundamentally change who we became.

Hedonic adaptation and rewiring the brain

So many of us fight tooth and nail to hold on to our sense of self inside our marriages. Marriage can leave us feeling trapped and lonely. I'm capable of all the things I want in a marriage: kindness and connection, fulfillment and vulnerability, presence, emotional honesty, and physical closeness. But I wasn't always able to show these things in the first version of my marriage.

My husband and I have struggled to reconcile his shame with my feelings. It's been a balancing act for me, learning how to not carry my hurt alone while knowing that my hurt triggers his shame. In the beginning of our healing, we talked about my feelings every day: how I was feeling, what I was struggling with, what I needed. As time passed, hedonic adaptation began to rear its ugly head.

Our brains make big changes after positive or negative events happen only to return, over time, to a baseline. This is hedonic adaptation.[20] In other words, we forget how badly we wanted to create change within ourselves because the crisis that spurred the change has settled and the diligence of self-growth has worn off. For example, when your marriage breaks and you desperately want your family back, you're one-hundred-percent invested in doing anything and everything to make that happen. One year later, old behaviors and old routines start to appear. Hedonic adaptation can be particularly troublesome when a marriage is healing from infidelity. One partner might move on more quickly, leaving the other holding the bag. Time, or hedonic adaptation, allows us to forget just how bad it hurt.

Understanding a little about how our brains work can help us greatly in creating new patterns. Rewiring the brain and neuroplasticity are relatively new ideas on the self-help scene. Thanks to researchers such as Dr. Andrew Huberman and Dr. Ginger Campbell, MD, the science behind creating long-term personal change is now accessible and digestible to everyone. While it was once believed that adults' brain pathways couldn't be altered beyond a certain age, science has now proven that even adults can rewire their brains to create change and build new habits. We actually can change the way our brain responds to our emotions.[21]

Learning why we do what we do from a scientific standpoint has been a game-changer for me in terms of managing my own mind. There are scientific explanations for how our brains control our responses, which in turn influence our feelings. When we learn about rewiring the brain, we can create a road map for how to change the parts of ourselves that are no longer working for us (for a few tips to get you started, see the final chapter in this section). Rewiring your brain and laying down updated brain pathways takes practice. A new habit isn't achieved overnight. We will get it wrong as much as we get it right.

Life events can force us to face new versions of ourselves. Sometimes with open arms, sometimes not. But with slow and steady work, we can build new foundations for ourselves and our relationships.

Right Time, Wrong Country

There are periods in life when everything feels so off-kilter, you reach max capacity inside your brain. Periods when you cannot process one more feeling, handle one more crisis, manage one more thing. Your eyes open in the morning and you instantly start running through the to-do list in your brain and life can't be anything but day-to-day because everything is debilitatingly overwhelming. These are the times when we forget to pick up children, forget that the mortgage payment was due five days ago, forget that we scheduled a counseling appointment . . . for three different family members on the same day.

It was in one such season that I inadvertently ended up flying to the wrong country and, hand to God, didn't realize it until the person who was supposed to be picking me up said to me, over the phone, after I sent her my location via GPS, "Jamie, you're not in Ontario, Canada, honey—you're in Ontario, California." Yes, in one such season of beyond-realistic pace, I'd landed in the wrong country and didn't realize it until my driver couldn't find me.

"How could something so ludicrous happen?" you must be asking. I damn sure was. How had I not noticed I hadn't walked through a customs line, or offered to show anyone my vaccination card, or in general not noticed I was flying to another state in the same damn country instead of to another actual country? Not possible, right?

Except there I stood, replaying every detail of the last twenty-four hours. It was by far the most out-of-body experience I've ever had. *Who the fuck am I? Where in the actual fuck am I right now?*

Just before hanging up the phone, having learned I wasn't only lost emotionally but also physically, I softly said to the driver, "I'm going to sit down on this bench and process this for a minute. I'll call you back." I hung up and looked up as if I hadn't seen the world around me for months—because maybe I hadn't.

My marriage had blown up, we'd torn apart our children's lives, I'd moved out, I was still running a company with a husband who'd cheated on me, my assistant was on maternity leave, I'd wrecked my car during a hailstorm, I'd sat next to my son while he had hand surgery, I'd released my first book and was having an identity crisis in the aftermath—I was basically a shell of a person going through the motions. I couldn't see beyond where I was. The future didn't bring me comfort because I had no idea what it looked like yet. And so I'd decided to go to Canada for a writers' retreat hosted by my publisher.

As I sat alone, in the wrong country, trying to piece together just how someone who successfully manages about six different schedules, who plans everything for her business and her family pretty much without fail, who prides herself on her organizational skills and attention to detail, finds herself in the wrong fucking country without realizing it along the way. Talk about a mind fuck. First, I cried. I cried about everything: missing the retreat, exploding my marriage, breaking my family, losing myself. It all came out in tears. Then I got in line, told my story, and asked for help—something I probably should have been doing a little more of in that period. Four flights and a two-hour drive through the countryside of Canada in a rental car later, I arrived at the retreat the following afternoon.

What I realized in the thirty-six hours of travel was that sometimes you have to get lost to find yourself. Sometimes you have to be completely alone in the world to work through your problems. Sometimes you have to open your eyes and realize where you are before you can see where you're going. This fiasco became all those things for me. I had my husband, my publisher, and my editors all offering to help in any way they could: find a flight, book a car rental, pick me up. While I was so grateful, I knew I was facing this part of the journey by myself. I knew I was going to figure this one out all on my own—I just needed a few minutes (or hours) to clear my mind and figure out how to take care of myself in that moment.

The myth of self-care

Everyone wants to talk about self-care and what it really means. Here's what I learned that weekend about self-care: It's not about doing the things that are extravagant or fun. It's not about the pedicures, the spa days, or the shopping. Self-care is doing the hard stuff we'd rather avoid. It's easy to distract ourselves by focusing on everyone else's needs instead of doing what will make us healthier. Self-care happens when we believe we matter as much as those we love. Self-care is taking care of oneself. I don't mean in a frivolous, surface-level way. I mean in a way that brings clarity, calm, and love into your heart. A little too flowery and woo-woo for you, perhaps? I know, it was for me too, for much of my life. It's just that the more experienced I get, the more I don't want to be last in my own life.

Self-care is the antidote to anger, resentment, anxiety, and denial. Self-care is making sure we see ourselves and our needs regularly and clearly. Self-care may be the bubble bath, but only if the point of the bubble bath is to lock yourself away and set a boundary with your family, making it clear that for the next hour, you're focusing only on you. Self-care can be the girls' night out, but only if you can block out your family and check in with yourself during that time. Self-care isn't about *what* you're doing for yourself—it's about setting and enforcing boundaries around your time and energy, so that you can do *something* for yourself. Self-care is about reminding yourself that you matter just as much as everyone else in your life. It's about pushing yourself to take that walk while the kids sit at home with their other parent. It's about making and showing up for those counseling appointments you believe you don't have time for. It's about scheduling that annual physical you've put off for years because every time it rolls around, someone else needs you more. Self-care is believing that you can and should come first.

As I sat on a bench in the wrong country, I acknowledged just how far one can stray from self-awareness. I acknowledged just how much of a toll keeping it all together was taking on me. I acknowledged I'd let myself become lost in my own world to the point where I didn't know where I was anymore.

That needed to change, once and for all. I needed to matter to myself before anyone else. I needed to check in with how I was doing before I checked in with everyone else. I needed to matter as much, if not more than, everyone I was taking care of. I needed to get a little more selfish.

I acknowledged that self-care meant having the nerve to take care of myself.

Ten Easy Tips for Rewiring Your Brain

You must have a daily practice. Yes, daily. Not once a week. Not every few months. You need to remind yourself every day of who you're becoming. Rewiring the brain is like working out. If you stop doing the work, you'll stop seeing the results—maybe not overnight, maybe not in the first few weeks, but in time, you'll lose the work you've done. Rewiring is a lifelong pursuit. Accept it. Deal with it. Own it.

Learn about gaslighting, emotional transference, and projection. These are the most common forms of manipulation.

Remind yourself often that another's actions aren't personal, no matter how personal they feel. Zoom out and see your life journey intersecting with the 8 billion other life journeys happening on earth. It's not personal—it's just someone with trauma crashing into you on your journey. Just as a car wreck isn't personal, neither is someone else's recklessness with your feelings.

Take responsibility for your responses to the world. You don't have to own someone else's actions and choices, but you do have to own who you become when faced with them.

Consciously choose how you respond to hurt. As bizarre as it sounds, we get to decide how we feel. Our brain is not at the mercy of anyone else. Don't let someone else's actions hold your reactions hostage.

Be willing to take the blame. Be willing to do whatever is necessary to create the peace you need. If that means being the one to call time of death, so be it.

Take care of yourself. Show up for counseling appointments, book annual exams, get in the car alone, tell people no, say yes only if it does you more good than bad, don't give in to guilt when it's time to do something for yourself, make time for your friends, let some things fall and break, and remember that not everything has to be your job.

Stop playing games. Stop saying things only to prove someone wrong or to make a point. Be straightforward and honest with others and yourself. Come from a place of good intentions.

Start asking yourself what you want to think about. You may need to take this minute by minute. I keep a waterproof notepad in the shower that says exactly this: *What do you want to think about?*

Stop stepping in. Stop doing the work for others in order to maintain a sense of control. Give up the façade—you aren't in control. You're being controlled by your emotions. Let others do the work they need to do.

SECTION THREE

The Broke Open

It is not easy to find happiness in ourselves, and it is not possible to find it elsewhere.

–Agnes Repplier

The Immaculate Caretaker

For the first forty years of my life, I believed that I alone carried the responsibility of teaching everyone around me exactly what and how to feel. After decades of therapy, I finally understand that my caretaking-martyr shadow-self developed as a result of my being raised by a father who drank and was mentally ill.

At an early age, I internalized the idea that to maintain any sense of stability in my life, I needed to take care of my loved ones. I learned to take care of those around me as a means of ensuring I was taken care of. If I woke my dad up on time, I could get to school on time. If I reassured him he was a wonderful father, I could keep him from having a breakdown. If I told him how much I loved him, I could help him end his breakdowns when they happened. If I met all his emotional needs, I might get some of mine met as well. I didn't, but a girl can dream.

Our childhood habits stick like Gorilla Glue to the rest of our lives. Children of alcoholics and mentally ill parents tend to take on care-taking roles as adults. From what I've learned, when we assume these kinds of caretaking roles, we're simply teaching our loved ones that they aren't capable of taking care of themselves, which results in a need to be taken care of. Thus, the cycle continues for generations. Old habits are hard to kick, especially in bloodlines. Instead of our immaculate caretaking skills inspiring others to create change for themselves, our caretaking eventually depletes us. Nobody wins.

It's easy to fall into the trap of setting up our relationships so that people need us. I was raised by a man who couldn't take care of himself, so I did the work for him. I continued the pattern for decades. Believing my value was based on how much I helped others, I created dynamics in which people needed me. This looked like overstepping boundaries as a stepmom, inserting myself into decisions that I didn't need to be making, and taking on all the day-to-day responsibilities of managing a household and raising kids. I did it all.

Then one day I was pissed off that I was doing it all. It can take years to realize we don't actually receive validation and love simply by placing the bulk of everyone else's responsibilities squarely on our backs. And once we do realize this, resentment and anger soon follow.

My oldest son once told me, when he was an adult child (because even when our children become adults, they're still our children), that when I worry about him, he doesn't live fully because he's worrying about me worrying. Honestly, I was shocked. It had never occurred to me that my caretaking could cause him to lose faith in his ability to grow. While we do what we do out of love, we caretakers end up taking away others' power to believe in themselves. By trying to do all the work for the ones we love, we rob them of the journey that teaches the lessons.

I brought my caretaking mindset into every relationship, including my marriage. "I'll care for you so well that you won't ever want to hurt me, and if you do hurt me, it's because you need me to care for you more." Ignore your needs and bleed for the person you love until you help them become the best version of themselves at a complete detriment to your own emotional and mental well-being. Right? Isn't that how the fairy tale goes?

Not quite.

It can feel good to try to manage other people's feelings—it can make us feel as if we're loved. But that's not what it means. It means we've made life convenient for someone else. They love the convenience of their life, and we become the vessel for said convenience. They may very well love us, but that doesn't mean we won't be taken advantage of as well.

My greatest fear is being unseen. I was a caretaker in hopes that I'd be seen in return. Seen, valued, appreciated. I'd spent most of my life feeling unseen, so I sought out those who were comfortable with me taking on the caretaker role. But inevitably, I ended up feeling unappreciated when no one could give me the validation I craved. Now I understand that I can see myself. I can give myself what I need. Now I understand that setting and enforcing a boundary doesn't mean I don't love someone. Rather, it's a testament to how much I trust them to follow their own path in this journey that they alone picked. Now I understand that I don't need to save everyone.

Zooming out

When we open our minds and take a look around, beyond the current situation, beyond the immediate moment, we can heal so many things we felt we didn't have any control over. Namely, our relationship with ourselves. My publisher and mentor, Sabrina Greer, calls this zooming out. It's the ability to zoom out from the small frame through which we typically view the world to see deeper meanings and connections. We can identify, for example, that a childhood spent taking care of a mentally ill father might just turn you into a forever caretaker.

I didn't know it was caretaking until very recently. I'd just thought it was how I was supposed to interact in my world. When I could zoom out enough to see that the dynamics in my marriage, in my family, in my life were simply extensions of a childhood with too much responsibility, I could start to change them. Caretaking is how I learned to be loved, so I didn't know there were other ways to love someone. I didn't know that I'd never feel fully loved by caretaking because we can never fully take care of the ones we love.

Along these lines, we can never fully understand what someone else is going through. So others can never fully understand what we're going through. There's no way around the hurt caused by betrayal. If our expectation is that the person who cheated on us learns to understand what we're going through, we'll end up disappointed. They won't ever be able to make amends in the way we want them to. At some point, we alone must carry the hurt.

Be it in the aftermath of an affair or in the marriage itself, our needs will not always be met by our partner, and we won't always meet their needs. The goal is not to meet each other's needs. The goal is to meet your own needs. All we can truly do is love each other, either close up or from a distance—whatever our inner peace requires.

Triggers, Triggers, and More Triggers

It's not just my husband who compartmentalizes things. If I don't intentionally filter out the thoughts sparked by things that trigger my hurt, they can grow and result in a full-blown emotional meltdown that prevents me from moving forward in any given moment.

Triggers show up as visuals, memories, even questions and can knock us off-balance in an instant. Sometimes a simple word sends me into a tailspin. *Eggnog.* The word is *eggnog.* I'll hate the word forever. Don't ask. The important question is this: How do we keep triggers from derailing our healing?

Triggers are going to come up. Thoughts will spiral. Especially in the early days after infidelity has been unveiled. You may find yourself sitting down to work from home only to spend seven straight hours poring over phone bills to determine exactly when the cheating started. Or going through the last nine months of text messages examining every "I'll be a little late tonight" message like a forensics expert. A certain level of obsession will take hold. I felt an almost animalistic desire to know exactly what happened, when it happened, how it happened, where I was when it happened, where my kids were when it happened . . . Trying to piece together the missing parts of your marriage can become all-consuming.

The obsession is hard to turn off. You might think that if you could uncover those last details, you'd find some peace. I'll break this to you as gently as possible: Even if you were handed a transcript with the entire truth and nothing but the truth, even if every single detail of the relationship between your spouse and the other person was presented to you, with no conversation left out, even if . . . even if . . .

You would still be triggered. You would still find yourself spiraling.

The who-stuck-what-in-whose-hole isn't the hardest part of an affair. The hardest part is the realization that someone else knows more about your marriage than you do. It's when you're thinking about the blind trust you put in someone else to make kind choices on your behalf that the thought spirals can take hold if left unchecked.

As it turns out, Who stuck what in whose hole? is fairly easy to answer. The questions we truly want answers to can't be easily answered. The physical act itself isn't what makes us feel unstable after we find out about infidelity. What we're really seeking is the why. Even if we never uncover this, we have a choice in how we handle the situation. We have a choice in how we manage ourselves. Do we stay with the obsession? Do we hate? Do we become bitter?

How do you want to come out of this defining moment? What person do you want to be when it's all said and done, five, ten, fifteen years from now? Perhaps the most transformative question to ask yourself is this: Do I love myself enough to grow and evolve from this life event?

When tragedy struck my marriage, after the numbing physical shock wore off, I was clear on the fact that this life event was no longer about him. Now it was about me. *Who am I going to become now?* I asked myself. *How is my life going to turn out now? What are my priorities going to be now?*

While it pains me to sound cliché, you really are the only person responsible for your life. Once you fully embody the belief that you are the only person in charge of your future, you can begin to manage the heartbreak that comes with infidelity. When you really learn the lesson, you find that the cliché doesn't feel cliché anymore. It feels like wisdom gained from experience.

When you own your power over your feelings and reactions, you feel less hate because it doesn't feel like everything is being done *to* you. When you get clear about who you want to be and how you want to behave in this very hard season of life, you no longer feel as if you have no control. Of course, you still have no control over anyone else's actions—the only person you need to manage is yourself.

So how do we manage the triggers without losing our goddamn minds? How do we show up for work the next day? How do we cook our kids' dinner? How do we answer the phone when our family calls? How do we maneuver through a life that won't stop even when we feel we've come to a standstill? How do we manage our lives when it feels as if we can't even manage our thoughts?

I was hit with a trigger the day we moved into our forever home 2.0, movers present and all. Said trigger (or in this case, the unsaid trigger) struck fast and hard. As something new and good was happening for my family, I was managing an internal meltdown the size of Chernobyl. I had to use all the coping tools I had: stop talking, start breathing, drop my shoulders (which I was holding about six inches higher than normal), and physically remove myself from the energy of my husband. Luckily, when you're moving, there's always another box to be packed or unpacked. I had to consciously and purposely bring to the forefront of my mind the person I believed my husband to be *now*. I had to trust in his ability to allow me to be angry yet again. (To be fair, something he's been able to do since doomsday one.)

When triggers hit, nothing but sheer choice will get you through these moments as the person you decided you wanted to be *now*.

In *You Are Not Your Brain*, Jeffrey M. Schwartz and Rebecca Gladding explain the role of mindfulness in mitigating triggers: "You cannot control the initial thoughts, impulses, desires or cravings you have—it is impossible to do so. However, you can and must choose how you will respond if you want to change your life and how your brain works."[22]

For most of my life, I fought the concept of "owning my power and managing my feelings." How could I (and why should I) be expected to control my response when someone else was clearly the reason for the response? Sure, someone else may very well deserve my wrath. But the more evolved version of myself also understands that ultimately, I'm always deciding who I want to be, and I do this through my actions and reactions.

Triggers are the rudest of uninvited guests. They pop up without warning. But since we know that they're going to show up at some point, we can prepare. We can make sure there's mac 'n' cheese in the back of the pantry, so to speak. To tame our triggers, we need to have a backup plan ready for when the day doesn't go as planned. Neuroscientist Dr. Daniel G. Amen offers a variety of tools to help manage triggers. He tells us we need to tame our "dragons," i.e., the "memories and events that still breathe fire on [our] emotional centers, driving [our] behaviors." He explains that we must eliminate the automatic negative thoughts that provide "the fuel for anxiety and depression."[23] Taming our dragons and eliminating our automatic negative thoughts may feel like lofty goals, but a little effort goes a long way. Familiarizing myself with how my brain is working in moments when I've been triggered has contributed greatly to my being able to better manage my anger and anxiety.

The more we learn about how the brain works, the more we understand that our minds and emotions are not our enemies—they can be molded. There are scientific terms for what's happening when we feel triggered. We can learn to rewire the brain and change the parts of ourselves that are no longer working for us.

Good lord I wish I had some magic wand that I could wave to make all the triggers go away, but we aren't living in a fairy tale. The only way to get through hard things is to feel the feelings, honor the experience, and decide who we'll become because of it. One tip for getting through the triggers phase of healing is to keep a list of long-term and short-term goals on you at all times. Long-term, maybe you want to stop having visual flashbacks, or maybe you want to go a full month without remembering something. Short-term, perhaps you want to go thirty minutes without remembering something, or make it through a full day without lashing out in anger.

I want to heal to a point where I'm no longer experiencing triggers daily. I drive through my neighborhood and have flashbacks that send my mind right back to the moment everything broke open. I still associate certain words, smells, and locations with the trauma of my family shattering. I'd like to heal to a point where I don't remember so much. The confusing thing is that when the anniversary of finding out rolled around, I realized I didn't want to forget everything.

I don't want a year to go by in which that day doesn't give both my husband and me pause about our marriage. I don't want one year to go by where we forget that we had the choice and we both decided we wanted to live our lives together. We both wanted to lay a new foundation. I don't want us to forget that our marriage is fragile and can be broken. I want us to remember that even if our marriage breaks, no matter the circumstances, we can still love each other. Still be kind. Still be able to honor all the good, even if it didn't last as long as we might have hoped. I want us to always remember that we're just humans walking this earth with a purpose that we may never fully understand.

Maybe the real challenge is to be able to manage the triggers without forgetting the trauma. Maybe healing means we never forget.

Maybe healing means we get to a point where we remember and simply let the memory pass through. *Hello, yes, I still know you, and I recognize how you helped me grow. It's good to see you again. Until next time.* And then we take our minds back.

Rechoosing Each Other

I was a Realtor for about a day and a half. I've waited tables, served fast food, worked for a district attorney, been a legal assistant and a secretary, managed a bank, counseled families in crisis, served as a research assistant, taught high school English, and coached a dance team . . . and subsequently quit all these jobs. My job history is a mile long, filled with full- and part-time gigs that for whatever reason ran their course.

I've walked away from people and never looked back. I've canceled on friends five minutes after I was supposed to show up. I've pulled chicken out of the freezer to thaw only to order delivery before the defrost button can ding.

I'm not afraid of quitting. I don't see giving up or bailing on a person or a situation that isn't working for me as a bad thing. I'm not afraid to see if there's something better waiting for me on the other side of change. While I've been wobbly when it comes to setting healthy boundaries, once a decision has been made rarely do I look back.

That's not to say I don't carry regret for every "wrong" turn I've made—regret is still something I battle regularly. I wish I'd been a better mother when my kids were younger. I wish I'd been more open to hearing what others had to say. I wish I'd been quicker to learn I don't have to say every single thing that pops into my head. I wish I hadn't spent so many years grasping for control to comfort me. Still, the more I understand and accept the idea of loving myself, the less I hate myself for every single misstep.

When I decided to reconcile with my husband, I struggled with feeling stupid for trusting him again. As mentioned, I once struggled to believe that marriages could come back from infidelity. I left fully prepared to leave my marriage. It's just that where things stand today, I don't want to.

It's not that I feel afraid of being alone, or of doing life alone, or of taking care of everything alone. I've done these things before. While I like being married, I wasn't afraid to face a life of singledom again. During the time we were separated, I quite enjoyed cozy nights at home alone in my little rental. Being alone has never left me lonely. It wasn't awful to have a few moments of not picking up after what felt like one million different family members every single day. It wasn't awful having the furniture exactly where I wanted it and the TV stations all to myself and the sink empty. These details may seem trivial, but the details can add up to the point where we don't remember who we are anymore.

As time went by and I watched my husband do the work of cracking open the decades of unlearning, I no longer felt that infidelity necessarily meant the end of a marriage. I could see how this thing—the cheating, the lying, the infidelity—was directly connected to how much he loved himself. The real question was whether we'd be on a reasonably matched timeline when it came to the hard inner work. Would our lives run at even-enough paces that one of us didn't always feel left behind or held back? Could we grow alongside each other while on our own paths?

The truth is we could have chosen any number of lives at different points in our past. We can also alter our course at any moment in the present. For better or for worse. The idea that my husband and I have rechosen each other brings me great comfort. I don't have to do this. We don't have to do this. We watched the previews of other possible lives. This one was simply the one we both chose, and we can choose differently at any time.

Perhaps other versions of ourselves exist and are living lives parallel to our current ones. Our souls are here to learn something, and nothing we do can stop that from taking shape, one way or another. The choices we make while here in this life, in this body, are simply how we're facilitating what our soul is here to learn. As overwhelming as they may feel, choices are just choices. So, if we don't *have to* stay married—we *can* rechoose each other forever. This freedom doesn't mean we don't believe in the sanctity of marriage. It just means our inner peace is allowed to be more important than the marriage. The marriage is the commitment to keep on keepin' on while expecting some derailments along the way.

Breaking up isn't the most embarrassing thing in life. Most of us can make a comeback after heartbreak. You get to choose the life and person you want to be. There's no shame in pulling the rip cord. There's also no shame in creating a marriage 2.0, or 3.0. This doesn't mean we keep letting people hurt us. While we maneuver our path alongside someone else maneuvering theirs, though, we might collide a time or two. That's just the reality of life. We then get to deconstruct and rebuild. Regardless of what that looks like for the partnership, it can be done without hate.

If making my marriage work requires me to be less present for myself and less aware of my own needs; if it requires halting my growth to make way for someone else's; if it requires more forgiveness than

I have energy for, my marriage won't make it until death do we part. I can make peace with that. It seems to me that now is the perfect time to imagine a world where marriage is a support system in our journey. A support system that can last for as long as we're healthy and balanced inside of it. Once we strip marriage of survival and obligation, we may very well open up a space that's better and stronger and more supportive.

Again, please don't misconstrue my words. I'm all in when it comes to my marriage, and I don't believe marriage should be taken lightly and walked away from if/when our needs aren't immediately tended to. This book could be considered a testament to how much I believe in the power of marriage. I just believe in the power of me more. Modern marriage holds the potential to be something it has never been allowed to be—purely a choice. It can be solely about choosing a life partner and committing to witnessing and supporting another soul in this human experience. After all, if we no longer need marriage to keep us alive, to put food on the table and to secure procreation, then what do we need marriage for?

Choosing not to quit

Spoiler alert: I'm no fortune teller. I don't know what the next twelve months or years hold for me. I know there will be ups and downs, and I can't predict what those will be. But I can focus on the things I can control. Namely, myself: how I manage my emotions, how I set my boundaries, how I challenge my growth. I'm choosing to focus on me. My reactions, my dreams, my goals.

I'm comfortable quitting a lot of things, but never again will I quit on myself. Quitting other things gave me the energy to start living for myself again.

I'm still invested in others' lives. I'm still working to grow my marriage and family. I just make sure I always have ten minutes for myself, just as I always have time for the other people in my world. Prioritizing ourselves isn't always convenient. Opportunities to take care of ourselves often show up at inopportune times. But if I'd give a solicitor on the street the gift of a few minutes of my time, why in the hell can't I give it to myself?

I want to be very clear about why I chose to reconcile with my husband. Why I chose not to quit our marriage. At no point AD did he blame me, shame me, or ask that I take any responsibility for his choices. He never backed down when I raged. He didn't gaslight me, and he didn't put a timeline on my healing. That's why we were able to eventually reconcile—not because I still loved him.

It's not about love. We didn't put the pieces of our marriage back together because we loved each other so much that love conquered all. Absolutely not. It didn't matter that he'd been my best friend, lover, and business partner for over a decade, or that we'd built a life from scratch, just the two of us carrying the weight of our world. It didn't matter that our children had merged into one family and loved each other fiercely. It didn't matter that we'd overcome moments of near bankruptcy, or that we'd created a life with each other we never could have dreamed of individually. None of this mattered when it came to the next step for our family.

I chose him again, but there would have been nothing to choose again if he'd given me anything less than everything. I don't mean that in a scorned-woman kind of way. If not for his ability to put himself in counseling, to face his mental health, to stare down his demons, to bravely face his abusive childhood, to set and enforce boundaries where needed, to fully look at himself and learn to love that man, there would have been no marriage to reconcile.

Forgiveness

Forgiveness isn't altruistic—it's actually a little selfish. Forgiving might seem like giving up, maybe even like quitting, but it's really accepting a new reality. It allows us to intentionally move beyond a specific moment. To forgive is to give up the victim mindset. If we forgive, we surrender to our current reality, and in doing so, we take back control of our emotional well-being.

Maybe we struggle to forgive because we don't really want to be responsible for our feelings and well-being. Maybe we sit in a situation for as long as we can without forgiving so that we don't have to own the next steps in our healing. No one else is going to do the healing for us, and forgiveness sends a clear message to the soul: *I'm ready to be responsible for my feelings.*

Is there someone you're not forgiving so that you don't have to be responsible for feeling?

Forgiveness can be a dark and lonely process. To forgive can be to go against every cell in our bodies. In her memoir *Finding Me*, Viola Davis defines forgiveness as "no longer wishing the past was different."[24] Forgiveness is about acceptance, so perhaps we're uncomfortable with forgiveness because we don't want to feel as if we're accepting someone's bad behaviors.

But what if it's not the behaviors we're accepting? What if it's the person? What if forgiveness is about seeing another human as a whole, not defined by any one action or behavior? What if forgiveness is about recognizing a lack of self-love in someone and using that recognition to love ourselves a little more? We've all heard it before—forgiveness isn't about the person you forgive; it's about healing yourself. What if learning to forgive others is part of the journey of accepting ourselves?

We can also give up the idea that forgiveness must be total and complete. Forgiveness can be fluid. It may come and go. It doesn't just show up in the yard as a seed and take root and flourish into a two-hundred-foot oak tree overnight. It's not a permanent state. Forgiveness is more like your favorite meal—you don't get it every day, but when you do, it makes your day that much sweeter. We wouldn't expect to eat only our favorite food, day in and day out. Yet we do tend to expect ourselves to reach some holy plateau of forgiveness and never need to forgive again.

The more we abuse our psyche by expecting to reach some arbitrary moral high ground, the more we end up hating ourselves for not achieving something no human can accomplish. Forgiveness isn't virtuous and it's not on some level of feeling that none of us common folk can reach. Forgiveness is scared and selfish and often runs and hides, just as we do. Let forgiveness appear when it can, appreciate those moments of acceptance and clarity, but don't expect to always live in such a state. Certainly, don't believe you've failed when forgiveness returns to the shadows to hide. That's not failure. That's progress.

Over the course of writing this book, I read a lot of books. I listened to a lot of podcasts. I went to a lot of counseling sessions. Aside from the counseling, the most transformative resource for me was Colin Tipping's book *Radical Forgiveness*, which really had very little to do with forgiveness as I'd always understood it to be.[25] I pray that I'm doing Tipping's message justice in saying that what I gained from his book was an understanding that every soul currently existing inside a human body is here to grow and learn and have a full human experience, and this often involves having certain challenging experiences with other souls. Tipping's description of spirituality helped release me from my victimhood and depersonalize others' actions, even when they flipped my own life upside down.

In my strongest moments, I can love myself so well that I know I'll always adjust and find my center again—as many times as needed in order to maximize the full human experience I'm so gifted to be living. I'll never quit on myself.

Butterfly Blood

Bias disclaimer: I believe there's no other way to heal than through counseling. If doing it on our own was a viable option, we'd all be doing it. When we're healing, we need a guide to help us. That's the role of a counselor. I'm biased in that I fully believe showing up to talk it out with a counselor on a semi-regular basis is a critical step when we want to change and heal.

During graduate school, I was pushed to ponder the question of whether humans must feel pain to emotionally evolve. The idea that we might be spending so much energy trying to avoid something that we should be embracing fascinated me. A professor once told us that every time a butterfly emerges from a cocoon, it releases a drop of blood—evidence that beauty isn't achieved without a little pain. The idea resonated because it allowed me to finally give meaning to all the pain in my life. I became staunchly convinced that one must experience pain to grow. In fact, I became so convinced that I eventually tattooed the sentiment on my body after a particularly rough period.

Today, I'm not so sure about the idea. I wonder if all the pain really was necessary. Does growth always have to hurt? Do we always have to bleed our way to a more beautiful version of ourselves?

Included in my college tuition were a number of counseling sessions through the university's psychology department. Eighteen years old and a new mom with little support, I took full advantage. I ended up with an amazing counselor, whom I saw until I was twenty-four. My relationship with this counselor and with the one I have now account for nearly all my personal growth and emotional development. For me, counseling has meant that every time I feel overwhelmed, unprepared to face an emotional interaction, or afraid to manage my feelings and reactions, I don't have to stuff it all down or compartmentalize it or ignore it. It's much easier to get through difficult days being able to set all the hard stuff aside and deal with what's right in front of me, knowing I have a designated time and place to pick up all that hard stuff again. Of course, that doesn't mean I deal with the hard things only in said scheduled time and space, but knowing I have this space has helped me balance growing as a person with getting through daily life.

The most life-changing questions I faced when I walked into my first counselor's office with a three-month-old were as follows: "What are you going to do about the lack of emotional support in your life? Whom are you going to reach out to?" The counselor's questions stopped me in my fuck-the-world-I-don't-need-anyone tracks. *Um, hey, lady, I thought you were supposed to be the smart one here. I don't have anyone else for emotional support—that's kind of why I'm here.*

She proceeded to tell me that she was very happy to be a part of my emotional survival kit but that she wasn't a long-term fix for loneliness. I'd need to seek out real-life mentors and support. I'd need to create relationships outside of this counseling office.

Well fuck. That's not how I saw this going at all.

Turns out she was absolutely right, and I'm forever grateful for her hard questions. She didn't give me answers—that's not the point of counseling. She helped me ask the questions I didn't know I should be asking. No one had ever told me that I didn't have to spend life on my own, struggling and emotionally isolated. The message I received growing up was much the opposite. I come from many generations of survivors. Nothing was sugarcoated and the truth was never dodged: "The world is cold and harsh, and if you aren't strong enough to figure it out on your own, you'll be swallowed up whole. The world doesn't owe you a thing, and if you depend on someone else, you'll be let down.

Period." Letting people in has never been my strong suit. Whenever I allowed myself to be vulnerable only to be abused and left, the truths of my childhood solidified. *Don't ask for help, don't be weak, and don't expect anyone to save you.*

Not only did I attend every individual session included in my tuition, but I also volunteered for the group counseling sessions led by PhD students in the psychology department. We volunteers were basically guinea pigs for the doctoral candidates, but I didn't care. I gained a tremendous amount of insight from those group sessions. Basically, every relationship dynamic each of us in the group had ever had revealed itself in this microcosm of our individual worlds, every shadow in our personalities. We had the opportunity to face ourselves—or to keep re-creating the same patterns for the rest of our lives. The fundamental principle of the group was that whatever your relationship dynamics were with the people in your life, they'd ultimately present themselves in the group.

I felt as if I were being given the opportunity to learn about how I contributed to my relationships and how I let others shape me—only in a group setting, led by a professional, with the intention of creating healthier relationship dynamics for the rest of my life. If only it had worked that quickly. I went on to have some highly codependent and unhealthy relationships and make some pretty derailing choices throughout my twenties. I also know those group counseling sessions helped me understand myself and others much better, without so much fear, even if my life choices for the rest of that decade would suggest otherwise. Change doesn't happen overnight. Getting to know ourselves is a lifelong journey, which is perhaps why we're so often overwhelmed by it all.

This second go with counseling has made me recognize how

frequently our toolbox needs to be updated. The very tools I fine-tuned in counseling during my twenties are the ones I'm now reevaluating for usefulness. When I was younger, I needed the anger to propel me into each day. I needed my impatience to take root so that I wouldn't get stuck where I was forever. I needed the chip on my shoulder to balance out the holes in my heart. Now, as a forty-two-year-old, I don't need the same things. I woke up one day and realized none of my tools worked. The ones I'd picked up in childhood were certainly outdated, and the ones I'd formed as a young mother and adult were doing more harm than good, but I had absolutely no idea what tools I needed *now*. Like my first counselor, my current one doesn't give me the answers to my life. Instead, she's the steady, thoughtful guide who holds the space and time for me to feel through the pieces of myself that are no longer serving me.

What I've learned through counseling over the years is that while I don't need to be saved, life lived with loved ones and a support system is more fulfilling. Of course, love requires us to risk being hurt and abandoned. If we never love, we can never be hurt, right? It's not that simple. Even if we chose not to love, not to expose ourselves in this way, we'd still hurt. Loneliness hurts as much as love can. Living life at arm's length, never trusting or being vulnerable with another person, hurts every bit as much as being abandoned when you do love. And when we can't love others, we can't learn to fully love ourselves.

Counseling has been my most effective strategy when it comes to healing my soul, learning to accept the things I cannot control, and being able to love who I am. I can't recommend it enough.

Not just any counselor will do. Not at all. Just as not every person will be our cup of tea, not every counselor will be your best fit. I went through several in my late twenties who didn't fit the bill for me: too quiet, too talky, too religious, too fake. A connection isn't guaranteed. It's our responsibility to decide if we can grow with this specific person. You may not be able to tell right away. Some may rub you the wrong way at first only to end up pleasantly surprising you after a few sessions. Others may offer an easy connection but won't end up offering the depth you're desiring. You're not obligated to a counselor or any mental-health professional. You are, however, obligated to yourself to seek out what you need to become the person you want to be.

At some point, we have to choose to heal. Healing is the step we usually want to avoid. If we know the fire is hot, we aren't going to touch it again. If we know healing involves hurting, we might just forgo the healing to avoid more hurt. Healing can be like sitting on a cactus—it serves as a resting point, but some spikes come along with it. We heal by intentionally facing the hurt so that it doesn't have so much power over us, but ultimately, we must choose to hurt a bit. We must choose to feel the spikes so that the healing may begin.

By "feel the spikes," I don't mean taking up residence in anger, rage, or resentment—a few of my oldest and neediest friends. I go way back with them. They're always up for a good self-sabotaging party. They also tend to bring uninvited friends to the party, such as hostility, insecurity, and hate. These things aren't what we have to push ourselves to feel. While it may be more immediately gratifying to hang with these "cool kids," we generally discover there isn't much depth behind their shells. Hurt, sadness, rejection, despair, and abandonment—that's what we're dealing with when it comes to healing. Sometimes we have to be brave enough to move to a new table, find a new crowd, and let ourselves take off the mask so we can heal.

And when healing, it's important to cry. Crying literally cleanses our bodies. Restores our cellular makeup. If we don't cry it out while in grief or pain, our bodies will not wholly heal.

Healing: The nitty-gritty

What does *healing* actually mean? That's a tricky one. Does it mean we never again think about the things that caused us pain? Does it mean we think about them but can keep our mind out of the spiraling state? Or does it mean we can look at the person who betrayed us and no longer feel hurt? All of these things can indicate various states of healing, but where we're at in our healing depends on where we begin and where we want to be.

Healing from betrayal happens in stages. The stage is determined by how well we're managing the waves of our emotions. We can get stuck in a stage of healing longer than we intend if we don't have power over our feelings, if we never stand up to anger and jealousy and politely excuse them from the decision-making table of our lives.

Healing is like painting a house. Everyone wants to rush past the hard work to get to the fun part: the paint-on-wall moment. The prepping, the cleaning, the taping off, the tedious work necessary for a better outcome isn't the rewarding part of painting. We just want to dip the brush in paint and immediately see the fruits of our labor. We don't want to be bothered with the mess and the prep work. But there are about fifty other things we should do before our brush ever touches paint. Most of the healing process isn't the paint-on-wall moments. Most of it is in the prep work, the boring stuff, the stuff that gives us a better product in the end. Putting real effort into our emotional prep work allows for a better healing experience in time.

Healing is like learning a new sport or language. It's not going to happen in six weeks. It can take many years to become an expert. But it might take only a few years to get decent at it. If you could be a better you in a few years, would you do the work? If someone showed you the path to a settled heart and a more whole, balanced version of you but told you it was going to take three to four years, would you be brave enough to say yes?

For me, healing has meant my mind is no longer ravaged by memories daily. I can talk myself off emotional ledges with some ease. My body is no longer physically triggered into numbness at the thought of the betrayal. I still have progress to make. I'd like to reach a point where I live every day unimpacted by hurtful memories. I'd like to continue to feel less and less emotional attachment to things I didn't know. I'd like to decrease the frequency with which I'm triggered. Healing for me looks like always knowing I'm not crazy, trusting my intuition, and loving myself enough to enforce the boundaries that make me a healthier person. I will know I'm healed when the infidelity no longer feels like something that happened to me and instead just something that happened.

I don't know what the future holds for me, my marriage, or my family. I only know that today, I like who I am a whole lot more because of the healing work I've done. I love that I'm breaking generational patterns of anger, anxiety, and self-hatred. I'm so proud of the human I've become, and I trust myself to steer my ship in any direction I need to fulfill my purpose here on earth.

My husband and I are both healing from decades of carrying shame. We're showing our children that it's okay to stumble and that what matters more is how you show up to fix yourself. I still don't know if pain must happen to grow. But I do know that if transformation is possible through hurt, then it's not our job to avoid it. It's our job to grow and heal from it.

I'd like to believe that as we gain life experience, maybe we don't have to hurt so much in order to continue growing into our beauty. I do know that we can come out better and stronger on the other side of hurt. I came out more in love with myself than ever before. And, in the words of Robert Frost, "That has made all the difference."[26]

Stop Moving the Lines

I've always wanted to write professionally. Becoming an author was the greatest professional accomplishment I could ever imagine. It's easy to tell myself to sit down and make writing happen. It's another thing entirely to do it. I often fight the writing by making up excuses or distracting my body from the paper it desires. I've come to appreciate that 75 percent of my writing process is just the brain talk required to believe I have anything worth saying. When I do get to the actual words-on-paper portion of writing, the words flow out, as though a pressure valve inside my brain has been released. When pen goes to paper, or hands go to keyboard, I instantly feel as if the cavalry has arrived.

Setting and enforcing boundaries can be a lot like my writing process. Seventy-five percent of the effort is the brain talk it takes to set a boundary, while the other 25 percent is the enforcing of the boundary. Setting a boundary can be like wishful thinking. The voice in our head says, "The next time this happens, I will/won't [fill in your blank here]." Setting a boundary is easy because it's hypothetical. Setting a boundary is deciding what you'll do when/if a specific thing does or does not happen. Enforcing a boundary is when you must produce. Enforcing the boundary goes well beyond brain talk—it's action.

A boundary is an emotional line in the sand. When we second-guess ourselves or are fearful about a boundary, it's easy to move our line when it comes time to enforce it. But the more you move your line to make room for someone else's, the more you lose track of yourself. I remember once exposing another of a long line of lies in my marriage before it broke and just not caring. I was so checked out emotionally that I'd stopped caring if my husband was lying. I felt no desire to confront him or talk about it. I just shrugged and went on with my day. I'd stopped caring enough to try. I'd lost the ability to see my husband as loyal and committed. I no longer wanted him, and I no longer wanted to be around him because I felt better about myself when I wasn't. I'd set all the boundaries in the world about how I expected to be treated, but I wasn't enforcing any of them.

Boundaries aren't what keep others from mistreating us—they're what keep us from mistreating ourselves. I spent years trying to prevent my husband from cheating on me, and it nearly broke me. When I look back on some of the journal excerpts included in this book, I can see how unaware of my worth I was. It hurts a little to read them. That person seems so sad and lonely. Desperate. Angry. Trapped. It's critical that we enforce boundaries so that we don't wake up one day feeling shame for how we've allowed ourselves to be treated. When we enforce boundaries, we're loving ourselves.

Know that there's a difference between boundaries and walls. A boundary is fluid. It can change over time. A wall cannot. Once a wall is in place, it might appear scalable, but the unseen shards will make doing so without injury near impossible. Boundaries can be worked through with mutual respect. Walls cannot. Countries have boundaries so that their resources aren't depleted. So should we.

Also know that the line of a boundary can become blurred when we try to treat people the way we want to be treated. In fact, I officially move to cancel the Golden Rule in all curriculums. Yup, I said it. Fuck the Golden Rule. It's a busted theory. The Golden Rule hinders our ability to set and enforce boundaries. Treating others the way you want to be treated won't result in your getting treated the way you desire. Similarly, others don't necessarily want to be treated the way you want to be treated. Haven't we all read the love languages book by now? Gary Chapman clearly told us the Golden Rule was shit. Okay, that's not technically what he said, but he did say that while it's our responsibility to pay attention to our partner's needs, it's also our responsibility to ask for what we need.[27]

The Golden Rule sets the expectation that we don't have to ask for what we want and need in life. We simply give to others what we wish we were getting. If I sound a little aggro about the Golden Rule, it's because I am. I worshipped the concept until it finally dawned on me that by giving people every good thing about me in hopes they'd do the same, I was putting an awful lot of my power in someone else's hands, and vice versa.

If we become dependent on others to give us what we need, and we expend energy giving others what we think they need, boundaries become very confusing. Who is responsible for whom here? Is our self-worth tied up in how someone else treats us? Are we to blame when a loved one can't love themselves? No. It's not our responsibility to deliver enlightenment and epiphanies to our loved ones. Boundaries keep us a safe distance from problem-solving on behalf of other people.

Boundaries are what keep us focused on ourselves, our journey, our growth. In her second book, Leisse Wilcox reminds us that "single, coupled, or somewhere in between, you are your own number one." She explains that "being alone has almost nothing to do with being single and almost everything to do with how we feel about being alone with ourselves."[28]

When we learn to love ourselves, trust ourselves, stop doubting what we know to be true for ourselves, we can truly appreciate that enforcing boundaries keeps us invested in our relationship with ourselves.

Put Your Anger in a Time-Out

For most of my life, I didn't cry over spilled milk. I screamed over it. I screamed at myself, my kids, my partners—whomever I felt was to blame for my anger. I became aware of the impact of my struggle with anger in my midthirties. Still, recognizing the problem is worlds away from implementing change. It's in a different time zone, speaking a different language.

When my husband's betrayal knocked me to my knees, it was the final blow to my anger. When the hurt came to find me, my anger simply ran out of places to hide. My anger was no longer allowed to make all the decisions in my life. In the midst of breaking down, I broke open. The anger I'd been carrying around my entire life just . . . deflated. Anger finally became something I could manage.

This isn't a story about breaking open and never feeling anger again. I still get angry, but my anger hasn't become rage since the breaking open. Not yet, at least. I didn't crack the code on managing anger once and for all. I simply learned that I don't have to choose that specific feeling anymore. I don't have to stay comfortable, forever bowing down to the will of my anger. I don't have to live on autopilot. I can take back the decision-making power when it comes to my emotions.

We truly do have control over our feelings. I don't mean in a com-partmentalize-your-emotions-so-you-don't-ever-have-to-fully-feel kind of way. We can change how our brains respond to our emotions in any given moment. In other words, we can rewire our brains. We don't have to let rage, resentment, anger, or hostility control our daily lives. We legitimately have the ability to slow our reactivity in hard moments. We don't have the power to avoid the hard moments, but we absolutely have the power to decide who we want to be when the hard moments happen.

Impulse control wasn't exactly a family tradition when I was growing up. The adults around me gave in to any and all emotions, every time they felt them, so I grew up having no idea I could say no to feelings that no longer served me. This means that for the better half of my life, when I was happy, I was only happy, and when I was screaming angry, I was only screaming angry. I couldn't see past my emotions to create different behaviors. I didn't know deciding how I felt was a possibility until I was forty years old.

We get to decide how to feel and how to react to our feelings.

Seems impossible. I know, I didn't believe it either when I first heard the concept.

Sometimes we need to put our feelings in a time-out. I mean a straight-up, toddler-style, sit-your-ass-down-in-that-corner-and-be-quiet kind of time-out. I do this frequently with anger. I actually say, "Little Miss Angry Pants, you sit here in this corner and be quiet because I don't love how you're managing this particular situation at this moment. When I'm done managing it without you, I'll come back and we'll have a talk about why your presence wasn't helpful here." After the situation has been handled, honor your anger (or whatever emotion is relevant) for all the times you did need it. Maybe anger helped you set and enforce boundaries. Maybe it propelled you toward creating the change you needed in your life. Honor it then acknowledge that you no longer need anger in the same way.

Maybe your anger doesn't need to continue your journey with you at the level of presence it once did. Maybe you've since learned how to lean in to other feelings. Maybe at this point, anger is holding you back more than it's moving you forward. Maybe your anger served to make you so strong that you can now comprehend other feelings, such as grace and love and inner peace. We can reevaluate our relationships with any of our feelings. Maybe it's time to let go of one or two, so that you can grab a feeling better suited for who you are today and the journey ahead of you. Your soul will thank you in time.

Just as an antibiotic taken too many times loses its efficacy, so will anger. At some point, anger no longer serves to move us toward the change we so desperately crave. At some point, anger starts holding us back from becoming the person we really want to become.

Maybe you're angry with me for presenting this idea. If you're angry because you can't yet manage your anger in angry moments, I say to you, "Of course you can't—yet." Allow me to pose this question: What have you done that makes you think you should be able to manage your anger in healthy ways? If you can answer with a specific list of techniques that you put into semi-regular use in your daily life, well, then you probably weren't the person who was just angry with me for telling you how to do something you don't yet know how to do.

In his groundbreaking book *Emotional Intelligence*, Daniel Goleman explains the science of our emotions. He writes that "temperament is not destiny" and that "our emotional capacities are not a given; with the right learning, they can be improved."[29] Feelings aren't as complicated as we make them. What complicates things are our defense mechanisms. We're often afraid to move forward without the emotions we feel have been protecting us for decades. But anger, shame, self-hatred, self-pity, jealousy, resentment, and any other emotion that's no longer serving your sanity and self-love can be put in a time-out—and you'll be okay.

Our negative feelings are like perpetual toddlers. They're never going to approach us rationally, apologize for the harm they've caused, and encourage us to move forward. Toddlers are driven by emotion. In the same way, the feelings that no longer serve us will continue to demand attention, and when they feel ignored, they'll lash out tenfold. They're not rational. But you are. Your adult, evolved, healing-centered self is fully capable of rational thought. You must ensure that the toddler understands you mean business. You must set and enforce the boundaries with your inner toddlers long enough to teach them you're serious about growth and change.

When you mess up and give in to the attention-seeking little scoundrels screaming in the corner (because you will sometimes), forgive yourself and help yourself be better equipped to follow through the next time a tantrum happens. The good news is you'll always have another chance. We aren't trying to banish any of our feelings permanently. We're simply allowing some to have more of a say in our daily choices than others. That anger ball isn't going to evaporate. The shame doesn't disappear into oblivion because we enforced a boundary with it once. Our tantrums are part of the journey to becoming the person we want to be.

Sometimes you'll get lazy, of course. Think of it like the Friday night when you just want to Netflix and chill but the kids are bouncing from room to room and won't settle down, so you let them eat ice cream for dinner and stay up on their phones all night long because you don't have the energy to parent. I get it. I fully appreciate Friday-night parenting. But if it becomes a habit, our kids will run the roost. We'll suffer the consequence of having kids who don't take our boundaries seriously, who don't listen when being spoken to, and who disrespect us. Lazy parenting of our children equals unruly children, and lazy parenting of our emotions equals unruly emotions that hold us hostage and prevent us from growing. There are no shortcuts. We can't ignore feelings and hope they go away. We can't enforce a boundary once and expect it to never be crossed again.

Responses feed emotions, so how we respond in a situation will impact how we end up feeling. The more anger we respond with, the more anger we'll feel. We don't have to carry the anger forever. We can, but we don't have to. We can set and enforce all the boundaries we need in the name of self-preservation. Sometimes the boundary we need to enforce is with ourselves.

We can put the anger in time-out.

I Know, Mom, Me Too

About nine months after the cheating was unearthed, while my mom and I were planning a visit, my mom sheepishly admitted to me that she was still mad at my husband. She hesitated to say it out loud but didn't want to show up at my place having not said it.

"I know, Mom," I said. "Me too." We both cried.

I knew she meant "While I'm hopeful for you, your marriage, and your kids, I'm still angry about how he hurt you all." I know, Mom, me too. But here's another truth. He is too. He has felt more shame than I could ever give him. The fiasco helped him do the work of learning to love himself more, but I suspect he's still working through forgiving himself.

That year, as our wedding anniversary approached, I didn't feel proud of our love in the same way, not yet. I didn't feel comfortable posting about our anniversary. I don't mean in the social media look-at-my-perfect-life kind of way. I mean not even for my closest family members and best of friends to see. It was also hard telling my mom we finally closed on our new forever home, telling my best friend about an amazing date night, telling my aunt about how our reconciliation was going. It was hard because one year later, things were going well, but not all that long ago, these people had witnessed me fall apart at my husband's hands.

They must think I'm insane, I thought. *Too trusting, naive, gullible.* Hearing the voices of my loved ones in my head, I tempered feelings of hope for our marriage to protect myself. Meanwhile, my husband was feeling gratitude for our marriage and freshly inspired by our relationship. It doesn't always feel as hopeful for the person still hurting.

The most obvious question after infidelity and reconciliation is "How do you trust again?" How do you trust someone who has proven to be untrustworthy? I've learned that trust is a conscious choice, and if you decide there's a marriage to reconstruct, then you must choose to trust again. More critically, I learned to trust myself.

My trust wasn't broken because I'd stopped believing him—my trust was broken because I'd stopped believing in myself. Today, I trust myself to never internalize someone else's behavior as a fault inside me. I trust myself to listen to my entire body when something feels unhealthy for me. I trust myself to manage the direction my life takes. I trust myself to put my soul's journey above anyone else's—not because I'm selfish, but because I'm the only person I can control. Doing so is a lifelong journey.

When reconciling after infidelity, we generally place the onus on the other person not to hurt us again. I'm suggesting we place the onus on ourselves. If we find ourselves in a hard place once more, we can walk away from victimhood. We can depersonalize the situation and confidently make the best choice for ourselves. We can live with the absolute understanding that we'll adjust our lives accordingly along the way. We can stop making choices that depend on what someone else may or may not do. We can learn to trust ourselves.

Another obvious question after infidelity and reconciliation is "How can you look at someone who hurt you and be willing to try again?" Remember, I didn't choose to give my marriage another chance because

I loved my husband. I do love him, but it's not about love. I was willing to try again because he learned to love himself. The most significant reason my marriage could be reconstructed is that my partner chose to deconstruct himself.

Regardless of how much we loved each other and our family, or how much we would have lost through divorce, there would have been no marriage to reconcile if he hadn't broken himself open. He didn't just make promises. In the aftermath of our separation, he put himself in counseling. He called the counselor, he made the appointments, he showed up for them, and he spoke his truths out loud. I had nothing to do with this. If I had, it wouldn't have been him fixing himself—it would have been me trying to fix someone else. Caretaking. I've done that, remember. I'm done doing that. My husband and I reconciled with different versions of each other. We are different versions of ourselves today.

Not only did my husband steer his own ship toward healing, but he also accepted every emotion I had, every time I had one. He never shut me down, he never diminished my pain, he never justified his actions, he never avoided the parts he hated inside himself. Based solely on these factors, our marriage stood a chance at reconciliation. His openness regarding both my journey and his is precisely why it's not about love.

In the throes of shame, humans can be paralyzed about owning their role in a betrayal. My husband didn't. It's as simple and complicated as that.

He doesn't love me more now than he did before. He doesn't love me more than someone else's cheating partner loves them because he took bold steps toward healing. We don't have some over-the-rainbow love that's bigger and better than any other love in the world and allowing us to stay married. There are also no heroes in this story. I'm not a hero for forgiving him, and he isn't a hero for becoming accountable to himself.

My husband loved me enough to face the decades of stuffed emotions, but he doesn't love me any more today than he did five years ago. My husband loved me before he cheated on me, and he loves me still. He just loves himself now too. And so, he can better love others.

Today, I feel an immense amount of pride for my marriage. I can't go so far as to say I'm fully grateful for the experience. I'd certainly have preferred we grow without such trauma. Still, having watched our marriage become something strong and supportive and safe, I'm grateful for who we are today as partners and parents.

Pura Vida

Travel has been a significant part of my personal development. What I've learned about life through travel is that no matter where you go, humans are just being humans, doing human things. We're more similar than we are different. We're all trying to figure ourselves out.

Even when I didn't have a dime to my name, experiencing the world was a priority. As a broke college student and single mother, I had to call in big favors so that I could travel—babysitters, loans, what have you. At twenty, I backpacked through Europe and stayed in hostels with my closest friends. At thirty, we did it again, but with slightly elevated digs. At forty, I had a vacation to Paris bought and paid for when COVID-19 hit, temporarily destroying my dream of sharing Paris with my family.

I've walked the links of Ireland, partied until dawn on the beaches of Spain, and ate crepes under the Eiffel Tower on New Year's Eve. But I've never been as moved as when I found *pura vida*. During the chaos of a broken marriage and in honor of my forty-first birthday, I decided to take myself to Costa Rica for a yoga and meditation retreat. If life is about timing, then Costa Rica entered my consciousness right on time, which is funny, because time isn't highly regarded in Costa Rican culture. More on that shortly.

Once I'd settled on a retreat location, I sat down with my husband, from whom I was still separated, and our sons, who were twenty-three and fifteen. I told them what I was doing to celebrate my forty-one years on earth, and then I extended an invitation to join me.

"Know that this isn't a vacation," I said. There'd be no room service or free Wi-Fi, no Netflix or lobby bar to retreat to. There'd be a simple cabin, tucked up in the jungles of Costa Rica, with a pretty badass view of the world. The experience would include three home-cooked meals a day, at specific times and not to be missed, a shuttle to the beach if coordinated ahead of time, and morning and evening yoga and meditation sessions, which I'd require them to attend should they choose to join me on the retreat.

This was exactly what I needed at this time, and if they felt they could fully participate and be open-minded enough to face their insecurities and grow a little, then they were welcome to accompany me on this adventure. To my surprise, they agreed. I'd known the idea of seeing Costa Rica would intrigue them, but I wasn't sure how open the three men in my life would be about downward dogs and "Namaste." Still, I felt hopeful for the first time in a long time. The boys were still working through the hurt of the family breaking up, and my husband was facing a lot of demons. We were all looking to become better versions of ourselves.

We arrived two days before my birthday, and my heart runnethed over at the sight of our two young men seeing life outside their only frame of reference for the first time. They didn't take one minute of it for granted. Everything was reason for awe and reflection. The four of us spent the next five days contemplating who we were and who we wanted to be. For the first three days, tears streamed down my face during the yoga sessions from the sheer emotional vulnerability of it all. By the end, we were all crying through our yoga sessions.

In Costa Rica, the phrase *pura vida* means "pure life" or "simple life." It's a philosophy centered around living in gratitude and not dwelling on the negative. When you enter Costa Rica, you take a seat and feel from the inside out rather than the outside in. The jungles offer shade to protect against the elements, the beaches offer fine-grade sand to exfoliate away the toxins, and the people offer a smile to remind you to slow the fuck down and take it all in—so much so that one night, we decided to have card readings done to find out what our spirit animals were. My card spoke so specifically to me and who I was that it moved me to tears. My husband and sons had the same experience.

My husband scheduled a massage for me with a local healer. Expecting a run-of-the-mill massage, I almost didn't want to go. Thank goodness I did. I left that session feeling a calm in my heart I'd never felt before. While much of what was shared with me in that session will remain private, what I will say is that the healer told me very clearly that I needed to let my sons go. She told me I'd done well by them and that it was time for me to let them go because if I kept holding on, I'd only hold them back. Having been a full-time, hands-on mother since I was seventeen, I felt my heart ache at her words, but I knew she was right. What I didn't yet know was that my stepson, the fifteen-year-old, was deciding whether to live with his mother full time, two hours away from us. Both young men were about to make some very adult decisions about where their lives would take them.

I've never wanted my children to have a life as hard as mine. In an effort to protect and help them, I've been overbearing and overly involved. I've overstepped boundaries, given them answers to their problems, and tried to shield them from every hurt possible. What I heard that day, when this Costa Rican mother and healer told me that it was time to let them go, was that I needed to trust them. I needed to trust that they were capable of living their lives without my constant overseeing. It didn't mean I was irrelevant. It meant I could let go. I could let go of my desire to manage their every need and start attending to more of my own. They wouldn't suffer, and I'd get stronger.

I'd already concluded that my husband's personal growth wasn't my responsibility, and realizing that the same was true when it came to my nearly grown children was a missing piece of my inner puzzle. I'd lived most of my years on this earth feeling responsible for everything and everyone around me. I'd only ever loved myself in relation to how those around me were doing.

While the role of mother often involves being a caretaker, a warrior, a doer-of-all-the-shit, the struggle is that for a lot of women, our families become our be-all and end-all. When we don't know who we are outside of our partner and children, we stop loving ourselves because we don't know how. When we sit in an empty house for two hours and can't come up with anything better to do than the dishes, we have lost ourselves. When we finally get brave enough to take a day for just us and end up back home in two and a half hours because we drove around and had no idea what to do or where to go, we have lost ourselves. When we don't know how to live if we aren't focused on meeting someone else's needs, we have lost ourselves. When we don't remember what kind of music we like, we have lost ourselves. When we don't see our strengths unless they directly relate to helping our loved ones, we have lost ourselves.

On an episode of one of my favorite podcasts, *The One You Feed*, host Eric Zimmer interviews Jack Kornfield. Kornfield, talking about what it takes to be a mindful parent, asks us, "Are you holding their bike or holding their waist? . . . Are you offering love or offering fixes?"[30] I was a mother who held their bike. I tried to be all the balance they'd ever need, tried to steer on their behalf, never letting them fall because it hurt me too much to see them in pain. My kids are so much stronger and able than I ever gave them credit for. Once I learned that, so did they.

When that healer placed her hands on my worn-out body, for the first time in my life something was wholly and only about me. A lifetime of deflecting my needs for the sake of my family's needs came tumbling down. I woke up parts of my soul that had been in hibernation for decades. I was introduced to myself as if we'd never truly met.

After the session, I met up with my husband and sons and couldn't get out words through the tears. I tried my best to explain the experience but did it no justice. Perhaps I'm not doing so here either. Still, the three of them somehow understood, held me for as long as comfortably possible, and then told me how much they loved me.

We committed to bringing pura vida back with us and returned from that retreat feeling calmer and more able to love ourselves. While we've all been guilty of allowing hedonic adaptation to seep in, we still frequently bring up what we learned about ourselves on that trip. Our boys not only remember four-wheeling through the rain forests, but also, the emotional breakthroughs we all experienced because we were willing to be vulnerable and honest.

A Conclusion

Like many forty-plus women out there, I love Oprah. I especially love her "What I Know for Sure" column in O.[31] I imagine O herself sitting down to write about something she's willing to tell the world—something she knows *for sure*. I don't believe Oprah is the kind of human who believes she's *sure* of many things. Someone who displays an ability to grow, evolve, and reflect, all while being an authentic guide . . . well, that's not a person who views the world as if she already knows it all. So, if Oprah Freaking Winfrey is about to tell me something she knows for sure, best believe I'm pulling up a chair.

It's in this vein that I ask myself "What's next?"

I'd be lying if I said I knew.

What *I* know for sure is that I'm still fighting some battles, and I've walked away from many. I know that if my world comes crumbling down again, I'll be okay. I know that forgiveness exists and that it isn't a permanent state of being. I know that bad things happen in good marriages. I know that I still sometimes confuse my hurt with anger. I know that I'll always be broken in some places.

Not everyone wants to see themselves as broken, but to me, being broken is a badge of honor. Unbroken things haven't lived. They haven't been in danger or harmed or scared or handled without care. My dear, if you aren't a little broken, you haven't really been human. Our souls didn't come here only to experience joy and happiness. They came here to this earth at this time as these humans because they want to feel it all, and to give them that experience, we must live. To live means we'll get dented, scratched, even broken.

My scars have changed me, and I'm okay with the reminders. My soul is here to experience everything living has to offer. Not just the easy parts. Not just the fun stuff.

I still don't understand infidelity. That hurt is not healed. I do understand that you can be burned by life so many times that you figure out how to hide, only to find you're simply hiding from yourself. I also understand that when you hide well enough, for long enough, it's really hard to find your way back. I understand getting stuck as a person you don't want to be and fighting like hell to become something different.

The infidelity in my marriage ended up becoming a spiritual journey for me. I've been guided through it: to write the words, to create the sentences. This book feels channeled. I felt as if the universe were talking to me, guiding me to the ideas. This channeling helped me to see myself clearly—something we humans so often struggle with. To see ourselves in any given moment is to begin the journey of learning to love ourselves.

In loving myself, I can accept that all my emotions must be experienced. What I can't accept is certain emotions getting more say than others. What I can't accept is hate and anger taking hold and squeezing out all the other feelings. By accepting my brokenness, some of which can be healed, I'm really accepting my humanity. I'm making room for other feelings. If I can honor the experiences that I've traveled into this body to live, I really am okay. I can feel it. And in the times when I'm not okay, I can do something to change it. Any time, any day. I have the ability to create a different path. When you learn to love yourself, you really can do and be anything. Those damn clichés again . . .

I missed deadlines for six months while writing this book. Every first of the month, I'd confidently inform my editors that this would be the month I'd finish the book. Only I couldn't because I hadn't lived through enough of the story yet. Now I understand that the journey I was writing about wasn't over yet. How could I finish a book about something I was still very much living? Now I also understand it won't ever be truly finished.

I finally did turn in a fifty-five-thousand-word manuscript. And when I received my editor's list of next steps, I swore loudly when I read "You don't have a conclusion." Are. You. Fucking. Kidding. Me. Who in the hell did she think she was? No, I don't have a conclusion. What in the actual fuck are you talking about, fuck you very much.

"Don't have a conclusion," I said mockingly. "Did you even read the manuscript in the first place? I don't have a conclusion because I don't know how it fucking ends!"

After calming down, I reread the to-do list and it occurred to me that my editor, bless her heart, hadn't actually said, "You fucking loser, how in the hell does your story end? Do you live happily fucking ever after or not, asshat?" Nope. Turns out all she'd said was "You don't have a conclusion." As in, please write one.

As I thought about what to write, I was reminded of something Esther Perel eloquently said about her partner and her: "We have had many marriages—to each other."[32] My husband and I have become different people, many times, over the course of our marriage. We continue to choose the new people. I don't know how this story ends. I'm happy today. I'm respected and I feel seen and heard. If one day I wake up and I need different boundaries, I'm okay with that. I'm not afraid I won't be able to handle something.

The conclusion isn't about the state of my marriage—it's about the state of me. What am I ignoring, hiding, dancing around, worrying about? That's for me to figure out.

The conclusion is that your life needs to be about you. Your growth, your healing, your self-reflection, your journey. My hope for you is that you walk alongside many people to love while on your journey, but that you always love you first.

With that, I'll leave you with this.

Five Easy Ways to
Love Yourself

1. Accept that you are your only soulmate.
2. Accept that you matter as much as the people you're taking care of.
3. Accept that you aren't here to do someone else's emotional excavation.
4. Accept that you need to enforce boundaries, not just set them, and that this isn't being selfish.
5. Accept yourself for who you are. Today. And then keep growing on your journey.

Acknowledgments

Desiree – Thank you for being my counselor, mentor, and spiritual guide. I love myself as a direct result of our time spent together, working on me.

Turf Paradise Bunko Group – Thank you for guiding me, listening to me, feeding me, showing up for me, and occasionally rolling some dice. I am so grateful for every one of you.

Badass Bestie Bitches Group – I am not me without all of you. Thank you for being my anchor for more than twenty-five years of friendship and sisterhood. Thank you for always reintroducing me to myself.

Sabrina & YGTMedia Team – This author journey of mine doesn't exist without the love and support of your amazing publishing team. Thank you for holding my hand, pushing me when I needed it, and making my words become everything I'd hoped for.

JJ – Thank you for showing up in a flash flood, no questions asked, just to be my friend.

Krista & Lori – Thank you for always reading my drafts, being invested in my writing journey, believing in me, and being willing to tell me when you love something just as quickly as when you don't.

Aunt Chelle & Uncle David – Thank you for teaching me what unconditional love looks like. Thank you for always showing up and having my back.

Mom – Thank you for showing me what a lifelong pursuit of becoming who you want to be looks like. Thank you for showing me how to be a fighter while also being able to love.

Sean – Thank you for never being afraid of any part of me. Thank you for never asking me to be anything I am not. Thank you for being brave enough to learn how to love yourself.

Additional Resources

Here are a few of the resources not specifically mentioned in the text but that have been critical to my growth over the last two decades. These are also the voices that have helped me through this specific part of my life. Perhaps you will find inspiration in them as well.

Books

Neale Donald Walsch, *Conversations with God: An Uncommon Dialogue* (G.P. Putnam's Sons, 1996)

Debbie Ford, *The Dark Side of the Light Chasers: Reclaiming Your Power, Creativity, Brilliance, and Dreams* (Riverhead Books, 1998)

Chandler Baker, *The Husbands* (Flatiron Books, 2021)

Esther Perel, *Mating in Captivity: Unlocking Erotic Intelligence* (Harper, 2006)

Elizabeth Lesser, *Broken Open: How Difficult Times Can Help Us Grow* (Ballantine Books, 2020)

Carol Tavris and Elliot Aronson, *Mistakes Were Made (but not by me) Third Edition: Why We Justify Foolish Beliefs, Bad Decisions, and Hurtful Acts* (Mariner Books, 2020)

James Altucher, *Choose Yourself: Be Happy, Make Millions, Live the Dream* (Lioncrest Publishing, 2013)

Dana Morningstar, *The Narcissist's Playbook: How to Identify, Disarm, and Protect Yourself from Narcissists, Sociopaths, Psychopaths, and Other Types of Manipulative and Abusive People* (Morningstar Media, 2019)

Natalie Goldberg, *Writing Down the Bones: Freeing the Writer Within* (Shambhala, 2010)

Dr. Bob Rotella, *Life Is Not a Game of Perfect: Finding Your Real Talent and Making It Work for You* (Simon & Schuster, 1999)

Maria Semple, *Where'd You Go, Bernadette* (Back Bay Books, 2013)

Isabel Gillies, *Happens Every Day: An All-Too-True Story* (Scribner, 2009)

Anne Tyler, *The Amateur Marriage* (Anchor Canada, 2018)

Justin Baldoni, *Man Enough: Undefining My Masculinity* (HarperCollins, 2021)

Podcasts

We Can Do Hard Things (Glennon Doyle)

Self-Helpless (Delanie Fischer and Kelsey Cook)

Lex Fridman Podcast (Lex Fridman)

How to be a Human: The Podcast (Leisse Wilcox)

The Man Enough Podcast (Justin Baldoni)

The Overwhelmed Brain (Paul Colaianni)

Notes

Endnotes

1 Leisse Wilcox, *To Call Myself Beloved: A Story of Hope, Healing, and Coming Home* (YGTMama Media Co. Press, 2020)

2 Michael I. Bennett, MD, and Sarah Bennett, *F*ck Feelings: One Shrink's Practical Advice for Managing All Life's Impossible Problems* (Simon & Schuster, 2015)

3 *The Good Place*, created by Michael Schur (2016–2020)

4 The Week Staff, "The Origins of Marriage," The Week (2015) https://theweek.com/articles/528746/origins-marriage#:~:text=The%20first%20recorded%20evidence%20of%20marriage%20ceremonies%20uniting,little%20to%20do%20with%20love%20or%20with%20religion

5 *Sex and the City*, directed by Michael Patrick King (2008)

6 Gabrielle Applebury, "Infidelity Statistics on Men, Women, and Relationships," LoveToKnow Media (2020), https://divorce.lovetoknow.com/Rates_of_Divorce_for_Adultery_and_Infidelity

7 Dr. Ana Nogales, *Parents Who Cheat: How Children and Adults Are Affected When Their Parents Are Unfaithful* (HCI, 2009)

8 Stephanie Coontz, *The Way We Never Were: American Families and the Nostalgia Trap* (Basic Books, 2016)

9 J. Vandeweghe, *Highly Sensitive Empaths and Narcissistic Abuse: The Complete Survival Guide to Understanding Your Gift, the Toxic Relationship to Narcissists and Energy Vampires and How to Protect, Heal and Recover* (Independently published, 2019)

10   Shelby B. Scott et al., "Reasons for Divorce and Recollections of
     Premarital Intervention: Implications for Improving Relationship
     Education," *Couple and Family Psychology* 2, no. 2 (June 2013): https://
     www.ncbi.nlm.nih.gov/pmc/articles/PMC4012696

11   *He's Just Not That Into You*, directed by Ken Kwapis (2009)

12   Esther Perel, *The State of Affairs: Rethinking Infidelity* (Harper, 2017)

13   Colin Tipping, *Radical Forgiveness: A Revolutionary Five-Stage
     Process to Heal Relationships, Let Go of Anger and Blame, and Find
     Peace in Any Situation* (Sounds True, 2010)

14   Jay Shetty, *Think Like a Monk: Train Your Mind for Peace and Purpose
     Every Day* (Simon & Schuster, 2020)

15   Teri Hatcher, *Burnt Toast: And Other Philosophies of Life* (Hachette
     Books, 2006)

16   Esther Perel, *Where Should We Begin* (podcast)

17   In his memoir *Man Enough*, Justin Baldoni explains that men use
     pornography to hide from themselves emotionally. "His brain tells him
     he needs to in order to feel safe, seen, wanted, or even loved." It's not
     about the relationship.

18   Malcolm Gladwell, *Talking to Strangers: What We Should Know About
     the People We Don't Know* (Back Bay Books, 2021)

19   Andrew Huberman, "How to Focus to Change Your Brain," *Huberman
     Lab* (podcast), February 8, 2021, episode 6

20   "Hedonic Adaptation and Eudaimonia," Dreameant,
     accessed December 8, 2022, https://www.dreameant.com/
     hedonic-adaptation-and-eudaimonia

21   Ginger Campbell, MD, "'Neuroscience for Dummies,' with Frank
     Amthor," *Brain Science* (podcast), June 20, 2022, episode 197

22   Jeffrey M. Schwartz, MD, and Rebecca Gladding, MD, *You Are Not
     Your Brain: The 4-Step Solution for Changing Bad Habits, Ending
     Unhealthy Thinking, and Taking Control of Your Life* (Avery, 2012)

23 Daniel G. Amen, MD, *Your Brain Is Always Listening: Tame the Hidden Dragons That Control Your Happiness, Habits, and Hang-Ups* (Tyndale Momentum, 2021)

24 Viola Davis, *Finding Me: A Memoir* (HarperOne, 2022)

25 Tipping, *Radical Forgiveness*

26 Robert Frost, "The Road Not Taken" (1915)

27 Dr. Gary Chapman, *The 5 Love Languages: The Secret to Love That Lasts* (Northfield Publishing, 2015)

28 Leisse Wilcox, *Alone: The Truth + Beauty of Belonging* (YGTMedia Co., 2021)

29 Daniel Goleman, *Emotional Intelligence: Why It Can Matter More Than IQ* (Bantam, 2005)

30 "Jack Kornfield on Inner Freedom Through Mindfulness," *The One You Feed* (podcast), October 26, 2021, episode 442

31 Oprah Winfrey, "What I Know for Sure," *O Magazine*, https://www.oprah.com/omagazine/what-i-know-for-sure-oprah-winfrey/all

32 Kate Hudson and Oliver Hudson, "Esther Perel," *Sibling Revelry* (podcast), March 17, 2022, episode 100

YGTMedia Co. is a blended boutique publishing house for mission-driven humans. We help seasoned and emerging authors "birth their brain babies" through a supportive and collaborative approach. Specializing in narrative nonfiction and adult and children's empowerment books, we believe that words can change the world, and we intend to do so one book at a time.

 www.ygtmedia.co/publishing

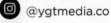 @ygtmedia.co

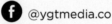 @ygtmedia.co